Isaac Schwab

The Christmas Motto

and the old prophetic presages of a coming golden era of peace

Isaac Schwab

The Christmas Motto
and the old prophetic presages of a coming golden era of peace

ISBN/EAN: 9783337092337

Printed in Europe, USA, Canada, Australia, Japan

Cover: Foto ©Lupo / pixelio.de

More available books at **www.hansebooks.com**

The

Christmas Motto,

and the

Old Prophetic Presages of a Coming Golden Era of Peace

An Inquiry

BY

ISAAC SCHWAB, Ph. D.,

AUTHOR OF 'THE SABBATH IN HISTORY,' ETC.

ST. JOSEPH, MO.:
PRESS OF COMBE PRINTING COMPANY.
1897.

CONTENTS.

CHAPTER I.
Discussion of the origin and primitive meaning of the Christmas Motto, " Peace on earth, good-will among men," and the author's own view on this point..... 1

CHAPTER II.
Extension of the argument of chapter I............. 24

CHAPTER III.
An effort to set right the famous prophetic visions, passing as predictive of a glorious, golden (Messianic) era of abiding peace, by an independent examination, with new light thrown upon different questions of this subject by the aid of advanced theological science............................. 33

NOTES.
1-40.... 65-121

EXCURSUS.
Treating critically of the prophetic enthusiasm about a blessed Messianic future, by illustrations from modern Assyriology, and partly with reference to Virgil.... 122

PREFACE.

My aim in the present work is to set in the light of critical inquiry the famous Christmas legend, "Peace on Earth, Good-will among Men," with the other half of the subject, as presented in the title, "The Old Prophetic Presages of a coming Golden Era of Peace." This legend carries an overwhelming significance to human society. In theory it is inestimable. But as yet it is a theory only; charming, captivating, effective in sense and expression, but yet a theory, waiting to be put into action. The same is the case with those prophetic forecasts of a glorious future of peace. They have thus far remained unfulfilled. They shared in the fate of all exalted and surpassing expectations for the future, which shine as castles with brightest hues along the horizon, but defy the human grasp. And the nearer to them people at times believe that they are, the farther they will in sober and thoughtful hours really find themselves to be. The happy and magnificent goal prognosticated in those olden prophets was never reached, however anxiously the friends of peace and kindly humanitarians were pining for it. Their ardent hope would never bring them nearer to it, nor bring it nearer to them. Were they thus disappointed? Certainly they must have been. But the repeated failure of their fond outlook did not weary and dispirit them enough to give it up in despair. This is, too, quite in the nature of hope. "It builds," as Pope says, "as fast as knowledge can destroy." Or, as Browning renders the thought: "All men hope, and see their hopes frustrate, and grieve awhile, and hope again." No disappointment could ever throw the firm Jewish Messiah-believers or Christian Millenarians off their track of hope, though they were disillusioned a thousand times.

As to the evangelical theory, "peace on earth," which has never yet been verified, it can surely not be said that this was due to the fault of its tenor. The trouble lies elsewhere. It is the nations of the world that set themselves against it and hinder its realization. They ever were and still are loth to incorporate it into their rules of conduct and mutual relations. They even refuse to be guided by one of the leading doctrines of the New Testament, which has equally with that theory been standing out clearly and distinctly enough these nineteen centuries past—the condemnation of warfare on the ground of the great virtues of forbearance and non-resistance. Strauss, in "The Old and the New Faith," relates that Renan had written him during the late Franco-German war: "Neither in the Beatitudes nor anywhere else in the gospel there is found one word promising Heaven for the possession or exhibition of martial virtues." This was undoubtedly a sort of sarcastic protest against the bloody war in which that great savant's nation was then involved. Who will deny that this protest was correct and well applied?

Formally, indeed, the nations accept that leading Christian doctrine. So do they avow the beauty and grandeur of the Christmas theory. But practically they do not heed the great lesson these excellent precepts teach. They have not the will determining them to carry this teaching into effect in their political interrelations. A further impediment to such accomplishment, even if all nations would consent in principle—as the more advanced ones really seem to do—would be the troublesome question, Who will make the first step and establish the precedent for such pacific course? It is evidently the solid concert of the nations in regard to the great end of universal peace and, in especial, an adequate awe-striking authority to guard this concert effectually from any wanton breach, that are sadly wanting. Possibly, too, such concert and efficient authority will never be attained.

It is no less notable a jurist than the eminent lord chief justice of England, Lord Russell, who, in an address delivered last year at Saratoga, rested his diffidence against the creation of a tribunal of international arbitration on that very ground.

While he strongly champions the idea of such arbitration, he yet urges this want as seriously hindering the cause of universal peace. In view of this circumstance, and also the point marked by him, that "most of the nations are armed," he is of opinion that a more sure advancement of this cause than might be looked for from any legal institution of arbitration, is to be expected from these more natural influences: the steadily growing and spreading public opinion with its condemnation of warfare and peaceful predilections, the ever increasing moral and intellectual culture of mankind, and in particular the pacifying factors of commerce, trade and travel between nations.

Assuredly, this view of the great English jurist, which we may, moreover, hold as largely representative of English sentiment at home, is not encouraging for the prospect of an authoritative and, thus, efficient tribunal of international arbitration being brought forth in the near future. However the people in general may favor it, it is their leaders and heads who, from a martial temper or selfish and sinister motives, take either an antagonistic or at least a dilatory stand in regard to the question. Too sanguine a hope may even not be advisable for us as to the point of arbitration yet at issue between the two great English speaking nations of the world. And concerning the other members of the family of nations, well—their standing armies are a standing menace to the peace and well-being of human society, so that at present little relief can be expected from a standing court of international arbitration, were it even that its creation was easy of accomplishment.

Nor, we have to fear, will all the peace leagues or congresses that may be held in the present days or in all future, help forward the cause of international arbitration and peace to any considerable extent. All such theoretical agencies will have little effect upon the absolutely warlike nations of the world. These will simply spurn or ridicule the idea of such theoretical bodies attempting to meddle in their own 'blood and iron' affairs. Highly praiseworthy as the well-meaning efforts of these associations truly are, their efficiency for practical good in a universal respect is surely questionable.

It is here in point to cite once more the above-noted writer, Strauss. Referring ironically to the notorious peace congress held in Lausanne, in September, 1871, he observes: "The famous orators, both male and female, who aired their sentiments at that gathering, should be reminded of Horace's suggestion, that the fashioner of men, Prometheus, mixed up the substance of the human heart with a portion of the fury of the grim lion." Then, taking up the point of modern evolution, he argues: "This scientific notion alone should have led those orators to the same conclusion. For, if man really descends aboriginally from the animal kingdom, he is primarily an irrational being. Accordingly, nature, cupidity and angry passion will, despite the progress of reason and science, retain great power over him."

Now that fable of the lionly admixture of the human heart need certainly not give us any concern. Different it is with that scientific problem of evolution. It certainly must set us pondering, and just in the direction pointed out by that unrelenting German critic. It cannot be denied that evolution opens a rather melancholy view of the outlook for universal peace. It inevitably suggests the thought that the gracious Christmas theory will, until a much "farther off" time, have to content itself with being a pious wish, a poetical longing. This time, too, will consistently have to be taken as coextensive with the indefinite and problematic period when humanity will have "thrown off the brute inheritance," which dates from the primitive, pre-social state of mankind with its peculiar military character. Whether or no the evolutionary conclusion can be verified, that "rivalry and conflict is the law of life," this much seems open to no doubt, that there is yet too much of the "ape and tiger," or, to speak with Horace, of the lion, in man's constitution, to let us expect a great deal from the modern expedient of a universal tribunal of arbitration.

"Man is not yet finished." Until he be finished, we may look in vain for the accomplishment of the old Hebrew oracle, that the time will come when war will be annihilated, and the nations will put away their tools of feud, vengeance or conquest and turn them into agricultural utensils. Until then, also, it will be illusory to expect a realization of the grand Christmas theory. It is readily seen and will as readily be conceded by all, that present and immediately prospective conditions jar yet too much with its sweet notes. Blessings of peace cannot be insured to mankind until the curse of war in the world be rooted out. That it is a curse, an unmitigated evil, despite some temporarily enjoyable inflation and a certain degree of progress in the sphere of human intelligence, no true man and well-wisher of society will dispute. Warfare is by all means a barbarous use, a relic of barbarity, which we otherwise so boastfully claim to have shaken off, and its cost, in every sense of the word, is incompensable. Until that happy event of evolution, when "man will be finished," there will indeed always be seasons of peace, yet its abiding golden age will not arrive till "men-murdering Ares" will be utterly put down and replaced by Isaiah's "prince of peace" (Isa. IX. 5)—in the transfigured sense of princely peace. Until then, too, there will also be breathing-spaces in the lives of nations, in which old sunny dreams of universal peace to come will be resuscitated with keen delight, and even lovely buds of springing peace appear to burst into bright and fragrant flowers. But soon enough they will prove themselves only feeble half-blossoms, doomed to ruin by new chilling blasts of cruel human temper passing over them, or scorched to death by the heat of warlike passion.

And yet must we not despond. On the contrary, we will indulge the hope that better days are in store for mankind, when within the realm of civilization the "fury goddess" will no more be permitted to be unchained and " march through prosperous lands, bearing terror and disaster in her course," but forced to be sitting forever upon the fierce arms, bound fast with brazen chains (see page 139 of the present treatise). We will confidently look forward to the happy time, however far off, in which fierce, cruel war will not be waged any more between members of the family of nations, but be held in abhorrence under the universally accepted sanction that it is "murderous to slay a brother man," in war no less than in peace; and when even crowned heads will no more be tempted, in their intoxication of power, to measure physical forces with other potentates, but will themselves shrink back with horror from bloody conflict as an unatonable crime.

It is not wise to offer a presage of the future. To gaze into its mazes with clear perception and descry what lies hidden in it, is given to no man. But at least an encouraging glance of what is ahead of mankind, we may catch by the way of reasonable inference from the present aspect of things in civilized human society. There is, we hold, strongest ground for the belief that moral and intellectual culture alike will henceforth advance steadily, and meet no more relapses into barbarity or half-barbarity, as was the case in the march of previous civilizations. There seems no possibility of such relapse in this our electrical age or henceforth. The present high development of culture and refinement of feeling must inspire us with confidence that its moral basis will never be shaken more within the civilized world. We may further take heart for the uninterrupted progress of the high and blessed cause of peace, from the present movement for international arbitration. Never before were the intelligent classes of society so zealously intent on avoiding bloody contests as they are now. Never before was the question of international arbitration discussed with such native fervor and pure enthusiasm as in our day. The Venezuelan dispute, more than any other previous American complication, has opened the eyes of the public to the necessity of allaying mutual national difficulties not at the voracious mouth of the cannon, but by the venerable, ancient canon of "and thou shalt love they neighbor as thyself" (Leviticus XIX. 18). This sacred maxim, they feel, is and ought to be powerful enough to induce dissenting nations to meet and compose their differences by peaceful means and ways, and fair and lawful arrangement. Since then the question of international arbitration has not subsided in vigor or lost in interest. On the contrary, it has grown and expanded more and more. The principle of such arbiration has found its noble embodiment in an existing treaty between England and America. All hail to the wise and patriotic diplomats who brought it about!

From this narrower compass of the great question we may enlarge our vista, and fairly regard it as the auspicious harbinger of that more general, even universal improvement of the times, when the law of love will practically be infused into the so-called law of nations, and these will of their own accord abolish pernicious warfare, and uniformly pursue a policy of peace and agreement, or amicable adjustment in threatening tensions of national feeling. Towards the attainment of this glorious, golden end all of us, individually and unitedly, must work with our best powers.

Let, then, no melancholy misgiving disturb our hopeful sentiment, but let us trust that humanity will henceforth and forever "move upward, working out the beast and letting the ape and tiger die;" and that all fierce rivalry will more and more decrease within civilized society, and only peaceful competition prevail, the password being no more, strive to hurt and wound, but "strive and thrive."

The present treatise deals with the problem of peace in human society, in connection with pertinent sacred texts. May it meet with many congenial readers ready to accord it a generous appreciation. It has been written in the spirit of fairness, and in the service of pure science merely. Dogmatic bias or prejudice never entered deliberately into its fabric. In return it expects from the public the same spirit of fairness in receiving and judging upon it. Looking forward to the *good-will* of the public, I now send it forth, commissioned to perform its task of helping to clear up important questions ever of interest to earnest Jewish and Christian minds alike.

THE AUTHOR.

CHAPTER I.

"Ring out, ye crystal spheres!
Once bless our human ears,
　　If ye have power to touch our senses so; . . .

For, if such holy song
Enwrap our fancy long,
　　Time will run back, and fetch the age of gold; . . .

Yea, Truth and Justice then
Will down return to men,
　　Orb'd in a rainbow;" . . .
　　　　　　　　　　(Milton, 'Ode on the Nativity.')

The beautiful Christmas legend, "Peace on earth, good-will among men," taken from Luke, chapter II.14, may fitly be compared to the glittering crest of a wave. It is delightful and fascinating to view, but when it subsides again into its even run it will necessarily partake of the nature of the pallid or turbid body of water from which it has risen. The same may be said of that sentence which popular thought and parlance have seized upon and appropriated as practically conveying the lesson of good-fellowship and charity for and on the accepted day of the Nativity. The sentence is indeed in its superficial aspect brimful of brightness and cheer. It carries a momentum of sweetness and grace. But when we examine it in its proper place and logical context, it appears at once as something different from what it is currently held to be—a well-rounded Christmas lesson. While it will even then not lose its exquisite beauty inherent in its abstract perception, it can yet no longer appeal to the sentiment with the rapture of a splendid phenomenon, or be held reducible to a maxim incorporated by the evangelist with the intention of instruction or admonition. As such, however, it passes with the unreflecting and uninquiring mind. It readily assigns the first clause to the doxology proper, and is content to take the rest as a call to mutual "peace and good-will," which the festive recollection of the Nativity is presumed to awaken on the annual day of its celebration. But upon thoughtful reading and search the relative text of the Christmas sentence as it occurs in the gospel, far from being a clear, sunny saying, proves to be one of the most obscure passages of the New Testament writings.

As regards its direct and only purport in the gospel, it is a representation of an angelic song alleged to have been intonated in the night of the birth of Jesus in the presence of some Jewish shepherds near Bethlehem. The song is one of praise to God from the beginning of the verse to its end. All its parts are organically coherent and bear exclusively on the historical point of the Nativity, as which alone Luke can be supposed to have embodied it in his gospel. And his only purpose can have been to produce an angelic testification and at the same time glorification of the new-born Jesus as the Messiah and Savior. This is indeed, for all we know, in substance the concurrent opinion of all the theological expositors who ever set themselves to deal with the refractory Greek text of our sentence which, moreover, has been delivered to us in essentially divergent readings.

That consequently, let us say, a decided difference exists between the learned expositors in the construction of the sentence, is very natural. We cannot go into an extensive survey of the expository opinions that text has called forth in the past. It ever proved a real 'crux' for the interpreters, and offered a wide battle-ground for the display of exegetical contention. We propose anon to present our own conjecture which, we trust, will not unprofitably swell the already existing large fund of speculation on the content of the doxology.

Preliminarily we feel tempted to say that we ought, on the whole, not to go with it into too stern a critical judgment. We should bear in mind—what we declare as so very important for the right estimate of texts of the kind—that it belongs on the one hand to the age of miracles and, on the other, to the age of uncritical use of and illogical reference to Hebrew Scripture passages.

The stupendous apparition and proclamation of angels would, truly, as the reported fact of Luke's gospel, offer no difficulty whatever to its writer or the simple-minded shepherds who are in it quoted as sole witnesses to that marvelous incident. Yet the sober thought of our scientific and reasoning age can meet it at best but with a reverent skepticism, and will consequently have to forbear treating it with the earnestness it is wont to bring to points of inquiry, verifiable or to be made probable at least by some sort of evidence.

Even in regard to the wording of Luke's doxology,

which is withal to be set down as having been drawn in some manner from Hebrew Scriptural patterns, our temper of investigation ought to be mild and indulgent. That the various writers of the New Testament were by no means particular with the form in which they reproduced old Scripture texts, can be proved by numerous instances. All they were concerned with was, to give authority and prestige to their own assertions or accounts by means of some accommodation to anterior accredited Scripture. However slight and insignificant this accommodation would appear to our modern analytical temper and judgment, it was to them all-sufficient for their present purpose, even for the general requirements of their time as well. And if the transmitted text would in its actual phraseology yield no support to their arguments or representations, they hesitated not to take the license of altering it to suit themselves. In this respect they went even far beyond the Rabbinic scholastics of those centuries, who would shrink with terror from the thought of practically altering any portion or relation of extant Scripture, even for the most pressing or most holy argumentative object. All they did whenever they wished to urge an important or curiously wise point was, to suggest hypothetically, and merely for argument's sake, "do not read (as it stands), but (as proposed instead)." A more common practice with them was to lean a proposition freshly brought out, against a few words or only one word of a Scriptural clause, however alien to their argument the literal and internal import of their quotation was.

In the New Testament writings we are multifariously confronted with Hebrew Scripture references which the authors thought fit to change, in the one way or the other, for the particular object they then mentally pursued and for which they sought authentic confirmation. Akin to this mode of proceeding there was another, which we wish to point out in support of our foregoing observation, that we ought not to apply a strict standard of criticism to Luke's doxology, as it is of a kind which does practically not bear it. We mean the formation of a sort of new texts from single stray passages of Hebrew Scripture, if no old one was ready to hand or could prove available to cover the point the respective writer would happen to urge.

We will in a separate note [1] illustrate this novel mode by some striking instances, and those of a character intimate with the Christmas sentence under discussion. Here we will state provisionally that we take this very sentence also as such an accidental new formation, gleaned from Hebrew Scripture passages that floated before the writer's mind, and then cemented together for the particular use of his narrative. How it may have come about in the mind and from the pen of Luke, (or the original writer from whom he drew) will later be presented. To judge of it thus leniently, instead of submitting it to a sharp exegetical scrutiny, we would candidly advise as the manner of treatment best adapted for it. This manner we must at all events declare preferable to the Sisyphus labor of coercing the text into unusual indications, to meet the various requirements of grammar and dogma combined.

Decidedly preferable it must be pronounced to the mode so general within conservative Protestant theology, to let the angels have forestalled the Pauline doctrine of Atonement or reconcilation of men to God through the death and blood of Christ. At this rather prevalent interpretation we now want to take a glance. We will first bring forward the exposition of Alford, the erudite English divine, whose Greek Testament edition enjoys an authoritative influence with the generality of our theologians. We have before us his sixth edition of the Testament. He divides, with many moderns,[2] the doxology into two clauses only, having adopted—since 1862, as he states in a note—the reading "eudokias," in the genitive. The "only admissible rendering" of the last words of the sentence is to him: "Among men of God's good pleasure." This good pleasure is however not to be understood as that which God has in men as such, but as that which he had "in Christ, by which he reconciles the world to himself in him (2 Cor. V.19)," The men of "good pleasure" are in other words, and those literally used by Alford himself, the "elect people of God." It is, then, not Israel as a body and a nation who were by the angels held in view as the beneficiaries of the Nativity, in so far that 'peace' (or reconciliation) between them and God would fall to their lot through Christ. No, the angels particularized in favor of the elect. And who are those elect? Obviously not even the generality of the future believers in Jesus' Messiahdom as such, as understood in Matt. XXIV. 22, but those predestined for salvation before the foundation of the world, in accordance with Paul's fatalistic position set forth in Eph. I. (cp. Rom. IX.) The upshot of Alford's interpretation inevitably is, that Luke made the angels from the outset discriminate deliberately, though only by implication, for the benefit of those who would eventually believe in the atoning merits of the death of the then new-born Jesus, that is to say, the elect.

But, let us ask, is such studied and rigid dogmatic discrimination compatible with the bright and pompous pronunciamento, as which Luke's doxology must strike every unbiased reader? Further, it must be objected, what imaginable good could it have done to the understanding of the shepherds to hear a heavenly host speak mysteriously in a language foretokening Paul's dogmatic teaching? They were undoubtedly with all the rest of their orthodox countrymen hopefully looking for a Messiah as the successful Redeemer from the yoke of foreign oppression. But we must emphatically dispute their capacity for making out the angel's supposable enigmatic allusion to Paul's later dogma. Their uninitiated minds could but have been puzzled by it, and even become worse confounded, if the point of election should additionally have been implied in the angelic proclamation. No, we protest, this construction of the angels having forestalled in their song Paul's twofold dogmatism of Atonement and election, has no reasonable foundation in the text. Not even the bare reference to the Atonement, without the sharp edge of predestined election, can be fitly imputed to the angels' song, for even that would imply a limitation to those who would eventually have unquestioning faith in the reconciling merits of the death of Jesus.

The angels, we aver, cannot consistently, from the whole texture of the story, be thought to have particularized in their song. This becomes more especially clear beyond any dispute when we take the doxology together with the preceding context, v. 11. Here the single angel who was first on the scene announced "good tidings of great joy to all the people," that is, the people of Israel—as Alford himself insists that the construction must be. Now the message of the single angel was avowedly and concededly for the behoof of the Jews as a body. Is it then in any manner reconcilable with such antecedent announcement that "the multitude of the heavenly host," who immediately joined that individual celestial messenger, should have differed from him so directly and glaringly as to use a language which implied proclamation of peace only to the elect few or the smaller number of "men of good pleasure," and these called so only potentially, in respect to their choice of belief in Paul's later developed dogmatic theory?

We will yet mention another popular theological work, in which the same dogmatism is presumed to have impliedly been forecast in the doxology. We mean Lange's Bible Commentary. In it the eminent American theologian, Philip Schaff, comes to decide substantially,[3] after some longer discussion, on the same exposition with Alford. He too ultimately determines upon the reading "eudokias," for the "weightier authority" it has for itself. And he construes the sentence: "Glory to God in the highest and peace (or salvation) on earth among men of His good pleasure." These are to him . God's chosen

Presages of a Coming Golden Era of Peace. 9

people"—Alford's "elect." To them, he reasons, God feels good-will or gracious pleasure, for their (eventual) reconciliation to Himself by Christ. For this sentiment he, like Alford, refers to 2 Cor. V.19.

The learned Farrar, in 'The Life of Christ,' keeps on the same line of Pauline dogmatic forecast, coincides in the reading of "eudokias," and translates: "and on earth peace among men of good will." Upon which Geikie, in 'Life and Words of Christ,' I. p. 560, observes very forcibly and pertinently: "the introduction of the idea of the elect as those to whom only the message of the Saviour is proclaimed by the angels is equally opposed to the declarations of God's loving the world, and to the grandeur of Christ's mission." We note this commendable opposition to the ordinary run [4] of conservative Protestant exegesis as a gratifying offset to the widely prevailing self-conscious pretension that the doxology admits only of the narrow Pauline construction.

No, we insist, with such dogmatic turn and aim the doxology would stand out as a graceless, forced, even harsh sentence, entirely incongruous with the circumstances into which it is set by the gospel writer. The scene as recorded purports to be one of angelic epiphany, at which unlettered Jewish shepherds were the only attendants. They could not possibly, we assert again, have fathomed the dogmatic mystery developed by Paul at a later stage. Nay, we fear no sensible contradiction in declaring, that no other Jew in the wide land of Palestine could have interpreted the doxology, when published by the shepherds, in a Pauline turn, as no one was then able to prognosticate this apostle's subsequent theory of Reconciliation as the aim and end of the life of Christ. Not that the angels themselves had not the gift or power of such prescience. To supernatural beings to whom the most unnatural things are possible, such foreknowledge, too, must have been a matter of course. Regarding the angels by themselves they could, then, certainly be most safely credited with a Pauline construction of their song. But as their message was intended for the understanding of the shepherds, and, subsequently, other plain folk, it must consistently have been couched in words which they could readily grasp and with the substantial drift of which they were familiar.

But yet from another point of view this internal difficulty might promptly be lifted. This is, that Luke's whole narration be supposed as having undergone at his hands a transformation peculiar to his own dogmatic position. Looked at in this light, it would indeed be quite conceivable that the doxology should bear a Pauline trend. Luke was unquestionably a Paulinist. He is therefore consistently expected to have written in the style, tone, and train of thought of the apostle whose system he had embraced. Paul's avowed doctrine was that peace of men with God was won back by Christ's sacrifice. This he laid down prominently in Rom. V, 1 sq. The theory is propounded in a twofold bearing in Eph. II. 14-18, where Paul dwells first on the peaceful effect of the sacrifice on the cross in drawing Jews and Gentiles into one, united, new body, and, again, on the reconciliation to God of this body of Christians newly

Presages of a Coming Golden Era of Peace. 11

made through that very sacrifice. On the supposition, then, that as a Pauline votary Luke created his doxology from his own mind so doctrinated, its sense would be about thus: "Glory (be or is) to God in the highest, and peace (with God is) on earth (viz., in men's spiritual relations, and in respect to their sinful state), good pleasure (from God is) among men." The last clause would suit well enough as a sort of amplifying parallel of the second. "Good pleasure" could be taken as corresponding to the Hebrew word chen "grace" or "favor," as used in Prov. III. 4.

ANOTHER PROVISIONAL HYPOTHESIS.

Having thus allowed provisionally for a Pauline dogmatic apprehension of Luke's doxology, it is pertinent to broach in this place the hypothesis of yet another doctrinal implication of that sentence, ere we bring forward our own interpretation of it. Let us remember —what is presumed by excellent modern authorities— that both Luke and Acts come from one and the same writer. Now when we compare the speech assigned to Peter in Acts X. 34 sq., we meet with an expression which bears also on the sinful state of man, yet is utterly free from the specific Pauline stamp of Atonement.

Peter is there introduced as speaking of God having announced "good tidings of peace through Jesus Christ."[5] These "good tidings" are, from the plain import of the context, no other than Jesus' preaching, from the outstart of his public career, of the same call which his relative, John the Baptist, addressed to the people: "Repent ye; for the kingdom of heaven is at hand."

Peter, we propose, may in his speech have understood the "peace" preached by Jesus either as the personal peace one has with his own soul, or, what is more likely, the peaceful relations with God coming through the new faith. In either respect he must have held before his mind, judging from his otherwise recorded doctrinal standpoint, the remission of sins [6] as giving such peace. And in either case, too, the peace attained through the message and mission of Jesus is, viewed conclusively, kindred to Paul's reconciliation theory: the difference between both apostles being only, that Paul makes the suffering and death of Jesus the means of salvation, while Peter sees Jesus' surpassing agency of salvation both in his life and death; for while living he preached repentance to his countrymen, and in his sainted state he continued to work remission of sins (see also ib. 43 and V. 31).

Now we think it supposable at least that Luke alluded in the doxology tacitly to the "good tidings of peace," preached by Jesus, and that accordingly his doxological phrase "on earth peace" (of which the subsequent clause is easily accounted as a germane parallel), bears the dogmatic sense of peace coming to sinners through Jesus, the new-born Messiah. To be sure, not much would be gained by such interpretation. It would be merely a substitution of Petrine in place of Pauline dogmatism. Against it, too, there would lie the same objection stated before— that the angels would appear as dogmatic reasoners, and with a message so ill-suited to the unprophetic mental capacity of the shepherds. This grave difficulty, again,

Presages of a Coming Golden Era of Peace. 13

could only be overcome by the view already above advanced, that Luke created the doxology from his own mind. Upon this idea, indeed, a Petrine no less than a Pauline tendency could safely be assigned to it.

OUR FINAL CONSTRUCTION.

After this preliminary discussion we will proceed to our own explanation of the doxology. We believe it to be a much more unlabored construction of its tenor, and to harmonize so much better with the temporal and circumstantial postulates of the whole narrative of our synoptic. We suggest in the first place, that this writer drew it from an original Jewish Christian source,[7] in which the event of the birth of Jesus was described in a brilliant and majestic style commensurate with the signal event itself. In it the epiphany of angels proclaiming the occurrence and intoning a momentous anthem in its honor, was the point of eclat which should prominently address itself to every hearer to whom the happy tidings would be communicated, and as well to every future reader of its record. The depiction of the scene proper, we remark, offered no difficulty at all. Yet a Hebrew Scriptural parallel, for which the author was doubtless looking as a model upon which to form his own composition, was not so ready to hand. While pondering to what suitable Hebrew illustration he might turn for the supply of a fit descriptive setting, he was, we surmise, suddenly struck with the adaptation to his purpose of Ps. CXLVIII. The leading antithesis, in this psalm, of heaven and earth being called upon to praise God, would offer an apt outline for his own brief doxological contrast of heaven and earth. For this first clause—the summons of the angels to themselves to give "Glory to God in the highest"—⁽⁸⁾ verse 1 of the psalm could be turned to good account. Then he would pass in his mind to the analogy of the psalmist's call upon the things and creatures of the earth, in verse 7, to also offer praise to the Lord. The contrast of the earthly praise the evangelist would consequently bring out in the two succeeding clauses of the doxology. The second clause would, conformably to that verse, have to be understood: "and (glory to God be) on earth (i. e. from all its creatures, for there is—incipiently—on earth) peace." The third clause would range fitly with the second, having likewise, as we will immediately show, a direct Messianic import. "Men" are here specified as the chief or rather, considered prosaically and practically, the only creatures from whom praise was due to God.

Let us, before we go on, state summarily that it is impossible for us to assume for the entire sentence any other reference than merely the birth of Jesus in his Messianic character, and in its Jewish national point of view.⁽⁹⁾ It is, we affirm confidently, a Messianic hallelujah, and purported originally to be nothing else. With this apprehension agrees perfectly the choice of the words "peace" and "good pleasure." The Messianic bearing of both is completely warranted in Hebrew Scripture, or, to speak more accurately, in that Scriptural phraseology customarily construed as Messianic.

"Peace" was in old prophetic passages as well as in

Presages of a Coming Golden Era of Peace. 15

the minds of later Messianic hopers, directly and closely combined with the reign of Messiah as Israel's future world-ruler, or generally with the longed-for golden era to be. How far Luke may have aimed to extend in his doxology the significance of the original Hebrew word shalom "peace," we have no means of ascertaining. On the other hand, it may be worth while to observe that the word bore with the ancient Hebrews a most comprehensive meaning. It signified so much more than a mere cessation of warfare or negation of strife. It denoted good health; freedom from care, chiefly a condition and feeling of security (cp. especially Isa. XXVI. 3); peace in every sense of the word; also kindliness, friendship and good-will; furthermore, as it seems, even peace of the soul in regard to human sinfulness (cp. Isa. LVII. 19); and lastly, prosperity.[10] The root-essence of the word "shalom" is total and thorough happiness in all respects of human life. It more often signifies weal or welfare than peace, in the sense commonly attached to this word.

Respecting eudokia "good pleasure" of the third clause, we think the original writer alluded to some such expression as the Hebrew shenath ratson "the acceptable year," or "year of grace," in Isa. LXI. 2.[11] In this place ratson "grace" has unquestionably an exclusively Messianic, or, to give it more correctly, redemptive bearing. The implication of the third clause would then be: as chief among the creatures of the earth, men are called upon to give praise to God, for with the birth of Jesus as the Messiah there begins a new era of God's "good pleasure in (or towards) men." The determining idea of the terse statement of this third clause is, that God has at last had loving compassion on Israel. He has relented to them in regard to the score of past sins,[12] his mercy prevailing over the stern sense and rigid measure of condign judgment. Moved by his mercy, he has now sent the long-expected Messiah. With his coming the eternal "year of grace"—the interminable golden age—opened for Israel.

That the tacit reference to sin should have been at the root of the leading thought of the third clause of the doxology is a supposition for which there could be adduced multifarious authentic evidence, alike from Rabbinic and New Testament literature. Let us remark, further, that according to our exposition the third clause would not really be an amplifying parallel of the second, but a kind of new argument explanatory of all that preceded in the sentence. The explanation consists in the point of view inherent in the expression "good pleasure," namely, that God, having now vouchsafed it to Israel, made it possible that the Messianic "peace" era, marked in the second clause, could at last arrive. Following out the words of the delivered text of the clause, we would have it understood: "(for) among (or in regard to) men (there is God's) good pleasure."

The whole sentence would thus prove to be a purely Messianic one. The angels were chanting God's praise and also calling upon the whole terrestrial creation to chime in with or follow them in his glorification, for the great event of the arrival of the Messiah which secures "peace" and betokens God's "good pleasure."

Presages of a Coming Golden Era of Peace. 17

The stress of the whole sentence rests however, we maintain, on the middle clause, which represents "peace" as the paramount signature of the reign of the new-born Messiah. Peace, truly, marked out pre-eminently Israel's hope for the Messianic empire. It was the very pith of their national expectations for the future. Its meaning was, as aforesaid, most comprehensive, and was above all that of security,[13] in particular, security from external enemies and the intermeddling and oppression of foreign powers. As such it formed, as it were, the key-note of the pathetic Messianic melody which resounded so intensely and fervidly in the unfortunate stages of Israel's history, when they were troubled by foreign invasions or became subject to foreign tyranny. As 'peace' was innermost in the consciousness of the people at large and cherished by them with fondest craving, so it became foremost also in the orations of their prophets, who were their spiritual guides and the exalted and sympathetic interpreters of their national feelings and hopes. We meet with it in the prophetic portraitures of the Messianic era to come, or the rule in it of the ideal king, as the predominant view of those inspired seers. They would inseparably associate it with the auspicious configuration of that fancied futurity, as its genuine and chief characteristic.

It will not be too much to bring for it some suitable Scriptural illustrations. We select purposely relative utterances of three contemporary prophets, as we believe that they are not only truly classical specimens of prophetic effusion, but otherwise best adapted to elucidate the point, that peace was the leading Israelitish conception of the character of Messiah and the Messianic era. Yet before we consider those prophetic passages we must briefly anticipate that we will later (in the third chapter) make out conclusively, and we regret to add, also disenchantingly, that the notion of the Messiah's rôle and rule of peace must essentially be modified, to be made to accord even with the innermost and rational presuppositions of its very prophetic exponents themselves.

Now when we wish to take a glance at the prophetic peace prospects of futurity, there naturally occurs first the well-known and often rehearsed picture of the golden age of universal peace. Both contemporary prophets, Isaiah and Micah, have so beautifully, nay gorgeously, with little divergence from each other, portrayed that ideal futurity in chapts. II. 2-4 and IV. 1-5 respectively. A delightful vision that was indeed. Possibly it existed already before their time in a fairly settled formula, and they adopted it for temporary purposes of teaching and lifting up the courage and hope of their countrymen. Fürst (Hist. of the Bibl. Lit. II. 302), following other notable commentators (Hitzig and Ewald), assigns that vision as the production of the much older prophet, Joel,[14] and holds that those later prophets took their glowing picture of futurity from this already previously extant source.

Now the essence of their prediction is, that Zion-Jerusalem would be the terrestrial center of Jehovah's world-dominion, a dominion carried on by the mysterious means of revealed judgments and instructions, issuing forth ever newly, as each case might require, from that central abode of his Presence. The revealed instructions—"Torah" in Hebrew, and probably apprehended in the double sense of commanding and teaching—would address themselves respectively to all nations of the world. These nations would, partly self-impelled and partly overawed by the majestic dominion of Jehovah, be moved to consult those Jerusalemite peace oracles. Consequently, implements and instruments of war would be useless and out of place in those elysian days of the future. (For a restricted sense, accurately to be put on the meaning of that bright picture of future peace according to the ultimate view of the prophet Micah, we refer to our note 14.)

The same sentiment is substantially implied in those prophecies in which an ideal Davidide king is expressly promised to come. Only that in these distinctly personal Messianic presages it is the Davidic potentate himself who will exercise the various central governmental functions. But, on the other hand, he is not to be understood as doing it entirely from his own mind and will. No, the wisdom and power of God pass to him by virtue of his sacred ordination (the outpouring of the ritual oil symbolizing the outpouring of God's spirit—and this spirit conceived in the intensity of immediate emanation and prophetic capacity.) This ordination, too, makes him God's plenipotentiary representative on earth. There arises thus between the terrestrial and the heavenly ruler a certain spiritual solidarity and mystical union, rendering the former's judicial and political proceedings as one in quality and substance with God's own decrees and acts.

Conformably to this settled notion we find in I. Zechariah[15] (ch. IX.) the peace rôle of arbitration, assigned to the ideal Davidide king, assimilated in its features to that of which the two before-quoted prophets, Isaiah and Micah, speak in their picture of the halcyon days to come. As in this picture it is God himself who as supreme Judge issues from his Zionite central seat his sanctions of arbitration between nations (Isa. II. 4), so will his representative Anointed of the future "speak peace to the nations" (Zech. IX. 10), from his central court in Jerusalem. This means that, his authority being world-wide, as it will reach "from sea to sea and from the river to the ends of the earth" (ib. v. 10),[16] his decisions of arbitration between quarrelling nations will prove as inviolable as God's own relative decrees are infallible and final.[17] And those decisions, too, are all inspired by his love of peace (or, what comes to the same thing, his principle of righteousness, as peace is by the same prophet (Isa. XXXII. 17) most truly said to be the outcome and product of righteousness). His pacific disposition is even remarkable in his public appearance, for he comes entering his capital horseless and chariotless,[18] devoid of any appurtenances suggestive alike of warfare and loftiness. In fact, all warlike implements would at that time be entirely extinct from the whole territory of Israel (ibid. 9, 10).

Let us view another kindred representation. The prophet Micah, a younger contemporary of I. Zechariah, who like him witnessed the disastrous Assyrian invasions, held out the coming of a new Davidide king "great unto the ends of the earth,"[19] who would be strong enough to cope successfully with Israel's arch-enemy, Assyria, and be himself "peace" (V. 4)—that is to say, his very name would stand for peace (cp. also Judges VI. 24). This ideal monarch would raise Israel into a mighty nation, dreaded by all others, so that they would no more have to tremble for fear of foreign intrusion and oppression. Eventually, then, horses and chariots and fortifications would no more be needed in the Jewish land, as all the aggressive foes would be cut off and all would-be hostile powers held in check and at a compulsory distance. Serene peace and sweet security would prevail at home under the potent sway of that august ruler (V. 1-10).

The prophet Isaiah, living in the same gloomy and troublous times of the Assyrian invasions, promised likewise not only an era of peace and rest from foreign hostilities, but the coming of an ideal Davidide king, endowed in the manner set forth in XI. 1-10. On the much disputed point whether Isaiah had here before his mind his greatly admired and highly exalted kingly friend, Hezekiah,[20] we cannot dwell. What we wish to mark here is, that the prophet delineated the glorious future Davidide as a marvel of a wise and powerful sovereign, under whom peace would flourish universally, even in the animal kingdom. In ch. IX. 5,[21] that prospective ruler is, among other illustrious appellations, denoted "prince of peace." It is further enunciated, that his dominion would be boundless alike in power and peace (v. 6).

The preceding illustrations may be sufficient to show authentically that the principal feature in the character of the ideal Anointed was held to be peace. The prophets had rendered it so, and there can be no doubt that the people fell in with them in those exalted hopes for the future. As time went on and political misery and social suffering engendered all the more intense cravings for deliverance, that fundamental feature must have presented itself and pressed forward so much more vividly, and laid so much stronger hold on the popular mind. Is it accordingly not fair to presume that likewise in the time of Jesus when, as we maintain on incontrovertible grounds, the high Messianic fervor had already run a course of well-nigh a century, the figure of the prophetic "prince of peace"—Israel's very 'pacifer'—stood out in the fancy of thousands of Palestinian Jews (the Sadducees, Zealots and, possibly, theosophic Essenes excepted) with the brightest hues of comfort and consolation, gleaming with quickening force over their national plight and misery? It was naturally the Messianic consolatory traits of peace, at which we might well imagine the desperate thoughts of the Jewish people would anxiously grasp in the woeful Herodian-Roman epoch of misrule, repressions and exactions. Peace—in the deep and extensive bearing the Hebrew word "shalom" had in the sentiment of the Jewish people—was never more needed than at that hapless epoch. Luke, then (or the original writer whose record he used), will only have given utterance to the very substratum of the Jewish Messianic hope, when he introduced in the doxology the thought of the newly begun reign of Messiah under the formula, "and on earth peace."

It proclaimed in substance that the long budded Messianic hope had at last flowered out with brightest bloom into that precious peace, which was the salient and all-important burden of prophetic promise in centuries of yore.

This our opinion that Luke made in the doxology no other but a mere Messianic allusion, and in the traditional point of view, may be supported yet by another circumstance. We refer to the expression "gospel of peace" in Acts X. 36. That it has an identical meaning with Luke's gospel of the "kingdom of God" is, we remark, all but accidental. It signifies to us that in the thought of the evangelic author of Luke and Acts the one concept was merged into the other, so that the 'kingdom of God' could stand interchangeably for 'peace.' By this kingdom was meant the Messianic. Under the technical appellation 'kingdom of God' (or 'Heaven') the reign of Messiah passed currently on the lips of every orthodox Jewish person in the century of Jesus. Peace, then, which was so markedly and generally identified with the reign of Messiah, presented itself so very naturally as the leading point of Messianic consideration also to the author of the doxology. The rôle and rule of Messiah were by traditionary conception settled to be those of peace. The doxology, for its part, gives expression to it too. We can consistently see in the whole sentence nothing but a proclamation bearing the Jewish national type. There will accordingly be no need of having recourse to the later theology of either Paul or Peter, to supply its internal motive.

CHAPTER II.

We have in this connection to settle yet another difficulty which offers itself to the careful reader of the New Testament. This is, that Matthew X. 34 sq. (compare Luke XII. 51-53) apparently runs counter to the peace rôle of the Messiah which, as set forth in the foregoing, is readily discoverable in Luke's pithy doxology. In Matthew (l. c.) there occurs the well-known passage: "Think not that I am come to send peace on earth; I came not to send peace, but a sword, etc."[22] This sounds surely like a warlike avowal! It must puzzle and confound the ordinary reader who, from his general knowledge of prophetic lore, can associate with the Messiah nothing but the rule of peace and tranquillity. Nay, more; it appears in sharp opposition to the picture otherwise portrayed in the gospels of the character and principles of Jesus. He passes notoriously in those writings as mild and meek and all but the bringer of the men-destroying sword. A glance at the Sermon on the Mount (Matt. V. 38-42) is sufficient to satisfy every one that a mission of strife and discord cannot consistently be imputed to Jesus as characteristic of his ethical position. And certainly is the application to Jesus of Isa. XLII. 1-4, made in Matthew XII. 17-21, strong enough evidence that the writer of this gospel had conceived of the Master as called only to the beneficent career of peace, and not to the agency of the tumult and violence of war.[23]

And yet is Jesus in the before-noted passage alleged to have announced himself openly and directly as a bringer not of peace but of the sword! How is this to be reconciled with the general portraiture of Jesus as the mild and peaceful Teacher? How does it particularly agree with the postulate, stereotyped in old Judaism and also strongly reflected, as we aimed to show, in Luke's angelic doxology, that the Messiah would be a ruler of peace, and its very personification? We can allay those glaring contrasts only by separating in our mind Jesus' ethical principles and the consciousness of his real, glorious Messiahdom, to be consummated coextensively with his second advent,[24] from his then preparatory career of the Messianic kingdom.

Difficult as it is to draw a strict line of division between the being and the coming of the Messianic empire—the Kingdom of God or Heaven—in the various relations in which Jesus dilates on this his leading theme,[25] we may at least logically mark off the one from the other. There seems indeed, in the face of those contradictory characteristics, no alternative but to make that distinction. We could then say: Jesus as the *initiatory* Messiah shared in the settled Jewish tradition—a tradition to be later illustrated—that discord is to prevail as a prelude to the Messianic dominance proper, but Jesus as the *future* and *real* Messiah could still pass as the coming peace ruler, and this according to the other prophetically derived Jewish stock conception, that the Messianic reign is that of thorough and lasting peace.

But, the reader will ask, can such distinction, involving the sharp opposites of strife and peace for the introduction and accomplishment of the same object, be at all sustained? Is it possible that a notion could develop in Judaism, showing forth the necessity of those flagrant contrasts succeeding each other in eventual history, in order to achieve the supposed Providential purpose of ultimately adjusting the national destiny of Israel? It would indeed seem, upon common reasoning, impossible, nay unnatural to presume a Providential design requiring grewsome contentions first, that sweet abiding peace might follow. But, in very fact, there is here really not the question of wise Providential disposition so much as that of arbitrary formation of dogmatic notions, propped by Scriptural references, however flimsy and far-fetched they might be. Who should think, we concede preliminarily to the inquiring reader, that a national body anxious for a long hoped-for mighty and glorious deliverer and restorer of ancient independence and prosperous enlargement, should have been driven to the extremity of cherishing that brilliant hope but in the gloomy shroud of dread disorders preceding its realization? But yet the Messianic problem has practically brought forth such remarkable incongruity. What we cannot reconcile in our minds has actually been welded together in the earlier centuries of anxious Messianic yearning. Thus it came that the image of a golden era of peace and bliss to come has been obscured by the dire specters of violent disruptions, both in society and nature, destined to occur antecedently to it. These in their nature mutually exclusive notions once formed, it was a slight matter, especially in times of desperate hope of Messianic accomplishment, to lean them severally on superficially construed would-be Messianic statements.

The incompatibility of these contrary notions may however, let us yet say, be somewhat reduced and moderated by the view, which we propose to make clear in the next chapter in a full and extensive discussion, that the whole expectation of everlasting peace attached to the Messianic government to come, had even no authentic and consistent support in the very prophetic compositions which bore the striking semblance of its indubitable and unconditional prediction. This point we have to waive here, as we desire first to show the probable cause which may have originated Jesus' utterance: "Think not that I am come to send peace on earth, etc."

This utterance, we suggest, was a sort of apology for his course of gaining disciples and adherents with apparent disregard of family ties and obligations. Whether or not he met with express reproaches for this proceeding in his Messianic career we have no means of deciding. But it undoubtedly involved a reproach, which we think he sought to extenuate in the discourse contained in Matt. X. 34-39. He did so mainly by advancing, in vv. 35, 36, the conventional Jewish assumption, that the Messianic times are to be ushered in by violent family disunion. This assumption, shared in alike by the orthodox Jews and Jesus, had its innocent source in the misapprehension of Micah VII. 6. In both the Talmud and the gospels this prophetic verse is utilized as the pretended signature of the Messianic prelude. Bewildering as it is to the modern critical mind to note the utter intenability of tracing a reference to Messiah or the Messianic period in that passage of Micah, it is nevertheless a fact that old Messianic believers resorted to it as a very mine of latter-day revelation. But the prophet's words contain positively no scintilla of such reference.

They are merely part of a scathing reproof the prophet was dealing to his contemporaries for their deplorable demoralization. Their degeneracy, as he indicates, had gone so far that faith had fled within the closest associations, and hostile attempts were made by the nearest of kin upon one another. Therefore the prophet held out to his countrymen the threat of an exemplary and decisive Divine judgment,—the "day of the (prophetic) watchmen, the visitation" (v. 4). Now Messiahists who scented eschatological presages in every prophetic rhetorical threat of a *day* of Divine chastisement uttered in the far past, seized also upon that passage of Micah and put on it the stamp of an oracular disclosure of a state of family dissensions to occur at the beginning of the far-off Messianic period. The testimony of such misinterpreting proceeding is supplied in both the gospels and the Talmud. Jesus had entered upon that commonly accepted notion, as is evident from the cited passage of Matthew.

It stood him in good stead, we propose, in accounting for or defending once for all his mode of acquiring followers. This was, his habitual demand to relinquish family relations and surrender wholly to himself and his cause. His repeated insistence on would-be disciples breaking away from the connections of kinship would, as already suggested, either directly draw on him or at all events imply the reproach of attempting to sunder deliberately the tender and affectionate bonds of family, and thus weaken the wholesome moral foundation of society. The defense of this his course we find unmistakably, though only implicity, intended in the cited passage of Matthew, X. 34-36. The trend of that entire discourse of Jesus, which runs to v. 39, we hold to be concentred in his reproduction and adoption of that passage of Micah, given in vv. 35, 36. And here, too, he stood on a Messianic track, well-beaten and familiar to his countrymen. He could readily be understood by his Jewish hearers. For, doubtless, the notion that the signature of the initial Messiahdom was domestic discord and disruption, was already then a settled tradition and a current orthodox formula. Jesus needed but to plant himself upon it to be promptly understood by Messianic hopers. And we assume that he purposely had recourse to it in the quoted gospel passage, to account practically for the peculiar manner of his propaganda. He meant to convey in that discourse of his, that his urging upon others to leave their families that they might "follow" him and help forward the kingdom of God—his own Messianic kingdom—by preaching it broadcast (see Luke IX. 60), ranged itself consistently with that fixed Jewish traditional presumption, that domestic strife was indispensably precursory to the Messianic empire. The warrant for his calling upon people to follow him regardless of family connections was thus given. It was in this sense that he declared that his (preparatory)

Messianic mission was one of the "sword" and not of "peace."

That he not only theoretically advanced the necessity of subordinating all love and attachment for parents and nearest of kin to the exclusive concern for his Messiahdom, as we learn from Matt. (l. c. v. 37), but practically urged the abandonment of family for his Messianic work, is irrefutably attested in Matt. VIII. 22.[26] This his exceptional position, then, he sought to attenuate by bringing forward that passage of Micah and implicitly referring to the current Jewish tradition based upon it. Surely, this tradition was not to the effect that the Messiah himself should by his speech and action bring about hostile estrangement in families and a renunciation of the tender ties that bound their members together. Yet Jesus referred to it nevertheless in his effort, as we suppose, at justifying his peculiar propagandist course.

As to this tradition, preserved in old Rabbinical lore, we are of opinion that it originally coincided substantially with the tenor of that passage of Micah, and that it only received changes and additions at different times according to the political-national condition of the Palestinian Jews. In the Talmud, treatise Synhedrin f. 97 (compare Sotah f. 49), we find already a considerably enlarged picture of the alleged dismal signs of the initial Messianic era: "In the latter days beginning the reign of Messiah," it is said there, "insolence will grow apace; human worth be debased; wine be dear despite its abundance (for the increasing debauchery); the whole (Roman) empire (including the Jewish land) turned to idolatry (or polytheism), with no one to check or

Presages of a Coming Golden Era of Peace. 31

correct it; Rabbinical colleges will be converted into houses of lechery; Galilee be devastated and the rest of Palestine desolated; the people of the country will wander about homeless from town to town, no one taking pity on them; the pious will be despised, and truth be wanting; youth will shame age, the son dishonor his father"—then follows literally Micah vii. 6.

This talmudical relation bears intrinsic evidence that it was gotten up into the present form in consequence of the woeful religious persecution of Hadrian and his strong efforts at paganizing the Jewish land. We may therefore safely date it at about the middle of the second century C. E.—when the remnant of the leading Judean theologians had settled in Galilee for preserving and cultivating the science and practice of Judaism. It is plainly seen that that talmudical relation is quite extensively spun out from its spiritual origin and stock passage, Micah VII. 6. But this does not concern us here. What we wished to demonstrate was that the latter source served alike to the Jewish doctors and Jesus as a sort of canon applied to the initial part of the Messianic times. In the Talmud a general picture of social confusion and perversion is elaborated from it, while Jesus has limited himself to its bare quotation for a countenance and, in a measure, for a plea of a prophetic precedent to his peculiar missionary proceeding.

On the whole, we may say summarily that the feature of family discord—Jesus' bringing of the sword —prevailing at the beginning of the Messianic period, was as much a dogmatic notion as the whole established trust in the eventual Messianic peace realm, so fervidly looked for on the strength of other prophetic announcements. Both were current side by side, and, though glaringly incompatible in spirit, were yet on curiously constructed prophetic grounds considered seriously and dogmatically as joint parts of one same scheme of expectation and belief.

CHAPTER III.

Here we have come to a pass when we wish to settle once for all, for the better and more correct understanding of ancient Messianic presages, a most important point. This is that all those glittering peace predictions of a so-called Messianic future, which we encounter in the olden prophets and which are yet in our days so very dogmatically construed as pregnant with the sense of the necessary ultimate cessation of warfare, were but problematic utterances of poetic enthusiasm and elation of spirit, with no more foundation of probability than what every other glowing hope for a better future supplies to their authors or cherishers. They were, let us say it emphatically, not inspired by any principle or motive of religious faith. They were in their nature and purpose national, and religious only in so far as nationality within the ancient Hebrew polity was never severed from religion. Yet while they bore such a national stamp merely, they are on the other hand to be credited with a high and excellent ethical merit of their own, in that those seers' true sympathy with the lot of their countrymen actuated mainly their prophetic imagination and intuition to produce and proclaim them. Much as the judgment of those worthy national-religious "watchmen" was, that their compatriots had themselves brought on the distress and misfortune with which they were now and then visited through their own deliberate waywardness and ungrateful disregard of their duties towards the God of their fathers, there burned yet in their heart of hearts the brisk and inextinguishable flame of patriotic and fraternal pity. This was so profound and ardent that it ever newly enkindled their zeal for lifting up the depressed spirits of the people, stimulating their despondency, and allaying their fears for the future, by holding up as offsets against indispensable vehement monitions and denunciations for evildoing, bright forecasts of prosperous conditions yet to come and be established.

It was, too, in a most unique manner that those prophetic preachers joined the threat of Jehovah's blasting visitations with brilliant visions of a restoration, even in multiple proportions, of former happiness and national greatness. This may have been partly modelled from the old Mosaic record, in which promises and threatenings alternate frequently in local position. Yet the mode employed by the prophets stands out as most peculiar in that both contraries are often not marked off from one another in a clear and readily perceptible way. At times they would even frame their severe threats by a sort of prologue and epilogue of such blandishing restorative contents (compare Isa. II. 1-4 and IV. and see Fuerst, 1. c. p. 45).[27] In some instances, as will later be shown, those presages of peace and bliss to come were uttered even in the face of grave political situations and social perils imminent on all sides. They could consequently mean nothing else than that such blessed times had to be bought at the cost of tremendous previous struggles.

Presages of a Coming Golden Era of Peace. 35

Peace, and peace in the ample sense of its equivalent Hebrew word, was to those devout preachers really but an indefinite eventuality, whether pictured with the vague outlines of the expression "in later (or "in the latter") days"—an expression most elastic and allowing of as much latitude of time as fancy might be disposed to clothe them with—or represented in some similar indeterminate manner. The fervor of tenacious and buoyant hope, cherished despite the most uncertain, even calamitous actual state of things, did not take into clear and serious account the possible distance of that consummation or the difficulties which had to be overcome in order to reach it. The consummation would consequently appear near enough at hand in the feelings of those prophets, though not in reality. Yet an indefinite eventuality, with an unbanishable element of precariousness beneath the surface of its prediction, this projective peace era must always have been to the most enthusiastic of those prophets.

An earnest and thorough inquiry will prove convincingly that the Messianic peace presages of the leading prophets Zechariah I., Isaiah I., and Micah, who lived and wrought in the troublous times of the Assyrian invasions, the second half of the eighth century B. C., had in the background a vast amount of warlike complications which lurked there menacingly and left little margin for the otherwise so ingratiating and enchanting fancy of a brilliant and enduring peace era yet to come. The Messianic king was in fact but a problematically eventual peace ruler. And no other construction can be put on the mere presages of an ultimate theocratic peace reign, in which no express mention of that terrestrial vicegerent of Jehovah is made (though this relationship and condition were doubtless always held to be implied in them). These presages, too, could have had but the meaning of an ultimate eventuality, before the realization of which there was ample cause for apprehending a various range of warlike miseries and fatalities.

Let us, to sustain our assertion, first cast a glance at presages of the latter kind. We have already above noted them. They are the famous peace prophecies of Isaiah II. 1-4 and Micah IV. 1-4. Precious sentiments those! Are they not? Yet we have to say, when we look at those charming lines in their local connection, they must lose all re-assuring effect by the contrast of war and its dire circumstances and effects threatened in the context.

Those of Isaiah are preceded and followed by vigorous denunciating arraignments of Israel[28] for their various unmitigated perversities (while, as remarked before, the denunciations of chapters II. and III. may, again, be considered as set off by the solacing epilogue of chapter IV.) A fearful judgment "day of the Lord" is threatened the Judeans in ch. II. 12, for their false worship, practice of sorcery, overwhelming self-confidence, and profligacy. This judgment God is to execute, as is indicated in ch. III. 25, by the visitation of destructive war.

While Isaiah pointed presumably in the denunciatory oration of ch. I. at the disastrous invasion of Judah by the allied Israelitish (Ephraimite) and Syrian armies under king Ahaz, about 738-34 B. C., which calamity was yet aggravated by the simultaneous hostile

Presages of a Coming Golden Era of Peace. 37

incursions of Edomites and Philistines (see 2 Chron. VIII. 17-18), there is, on the other hand, good reason to believe that in the denunciations of chapters II. and III. that calamity is not the only one to which allusion is made. The threat of that awful "day of the Lord" can have already implied in the prophet's mind the apprehension of the terrible scourge of an Assyrian invasion, supposably indicated in ch. V. 26-30, and expressly brought forward in ch. VII. 17, 20-25, and again in ch. VIII. 6 sq. That this apprehension was already then not distant from his thought may be judged from the circumstance, that he had witnessed from a youth the avalanche-like increase of the Assyrian great-power, especially under the "destroyer of nations," Tiglath-Pileser.[29] Whether or not it can be made out from several extant cuneiform inscriptions that the Judean king Uzziah was an eminent participant in the war of coalition against that mighty lord beyond the Tigris, in the year B. C. 742,[30] (which had a disastrous issue for all the confederates, though Uzziah may have preserved his independence), yet this much we can set down as certain that Isaiah had already at an early period been impressed with the grave perils to which all the western Asiatic countries, including Israel-Judah, were exposed from the ambitious and rapacious "Assur." That this impression had gradually gained hold of his mind is evident from his free statement, that Assur was the "rod of the wrath" of Jehovah (X. 5), appointed as instrument to chastise all who would incur it, Heathens and Israelites alike.[31]

Now as we may, further, fairly assume with the learned lexicographer and commentator Gesenius, that chapter V. of Isaiah was written about the same time with the preceding ones (see also our note 28), we are all the more justified in detecting already in the threat of the "day of the Lord" in ch. II. 12, an allusion, in a general manner, to punishing warlike aggressions of Judah by Assyria. Unquestionably, however, a definite reference can rationally be fixed only to the earlier trouble which came upon Judah from this source, that is, the oppressive tributary dependence on the great-king Tiglath Pileser, into which king Ahaz brought his country by calling him to assistance against the before-noted Israelitish-Syrian allies, ca. 734. While Tiglath-Pileser came as an ostensible friend of the Judean king, yet the relief he tendered was a most dear acquisition. It was purchased at an enormous price, as the Assyrian despot exacted a stupendous compensation which was attended, too, by Ahaz' sacrilegious spoilation of the temple and its closing to the worship of the God of Israel (2 Chr. XXVIII. 20 sq.) Surely, these sad occurrences, so far as they are attributable to the great-king, cannot in the least be taken as coinciding with the sense of Isa. III. 25, where actual war is threatened. This Tiglath-Pileser did certainly not attempt upon Judah. Yet while they may not be accounted as under the head of that war threat, they can fitly be considered as coming within the range of the judgment "day of the Lord," in ch. II. 12. For a severe and heavy enough visitation they were indeed, as can clearly be seen from 2 Chr. 1. c. Gesenius (Commentary p. 270) suggests already properly, that the misery resulting from Ahaz' appeal to Tiglath-Pileser for assistance was similar to woes of war, as the "tributary dependence on Assyria was the signal for a series of calamitous events." Yet for all that a definite reference can, as already remarked, be discovered in Isaiah's denunciatory orations of chapters II. and III. only to the ruinous invasion of Judah by the before-mentioned allies. The havoc they made all over the Judean land was enormous (see Isa. VII. 2; 2 Kings XVI; 2 Chr. l. c.) The hostile onsets of the Philistines and Edomites who turned its sad plight to account, added only to the general suffering and distress. Jerusalem only was spared (compare Isa. I. 8), and this probably because the opportune arrival of the Assyrian auxiliary forces averted its siege.

We have in the foregoing tried to track out as much as might be, and thus necessarily at some length, the compass of the mental attitude and vision of the prophet in conceiving and framing the denunciatory oracles of chapters II. and III., and, in particular, the main threat of the judgment "day of the Lord," directly denounced in ch. II. 12. For on the establishment of the greater extent of this threat than would appear on the surface, and its greater intensity, will depend the strength of our argument to be immediately brought forward.

Now we have seen, let us state it summarily, as admitting of no question, that that threatened judgment pointed to the dire calamity of the Syro-Israelitish war. But we believe to have also made very probable that this together with the threat of a fatal war to be visited on the Judeans, in ch. III. 25, involved besides, in the prophet's apprehensive intuition at least, warlike tribulations to be inflicted by Assyria.

The picture, then, reflected to us from the prophet's denunciatory chapters II. and III. is a decidedly and intensely gloomy one of terrible war and destruction. When we in the survey of this picture combine with its definite awful strokes the more or less indistinct, yet, as we think, fairly traceable hints of woe threatened to befall the Judeans, and then hold over against it the bright and pompous enunciation of a coming era of theocratic power, peace and bliss, at the head of chapter II., what a glaring and utterly irreconcilable contrast meets our view![32] Gainsay it, if you will, but we for our part cannot but insist that these precious sentiments of splendid and proud promise uttered before Judean hearers must, as the oration advanced, have been pitifully drowned in the dismal din of the weird denunciations, in particular the startling prophetic forecast of a destructive war (or wars) impending upon them. Jehovah himself, who is supposed to have inspired that initial sweet oracle, is later represented (in chapters V. 26, VII. 18, and VIII. 7, which are surely connected in sense and more or less in time with chapters II. and III.), as having purposed to rouse foreign powers to warlike visitations upon his people. But aside from this later representation, the mere threat of coming war could not consistently with the settled principles of Hebrew religious faith be understood as other than designed and directed by Jehovah,—as his Providence was from of old, in written and in spoken words, taught to comprise every event, even the minutest accident. And when we further and particularly consider that in the apprehensive vision of the prophet there stood vividly already when he brought forth and delivered the denunciatory discourses of chapters II. and III, the dread and blasting scourge of Assyria's great-power, what an exceedingly cruel contrast is offered in them with that sparkling peace paragraph at the head! After listening for a few moments to these few luring lines, the Judean hearers must have been suddenly seized with poignant amazement and shaken to the very depth of their souls, when the prophet started thence upon his opposite line of denunciatory declamations. They must have thought to themselves that that previous glowing promise was but a hazy apparition, purposely held out to vex and abash them, and a striking travesty rather than a quickening reassurance. For there could be no possible reconcilation of the contrast, created by those contrary sentiments in their minds.

It may be objected that the prophet had not spoken of that bright and happy era as coming immediately or after a short time, but had chosen the indefinite expression of "later (or "latter") days," and these might be far off. But, we must reply, had the hearers really construed those words of big promise as bearing upon the far or farther future, the contrast must have been no less sharp and chafing. For, they must have reasoned, what boots it that such glorious and blissful times will be ahead for the nation as such, if we, the present generation, are doomed to severe, even ruinous visitations?

But we have not done our questioning. There lies another grave objection against that initial peace paragraph, which rises unavoidably as we are to estimate clearly its acceptibility in a rational view, or only judge of it as having had any real meaning at all. We ask, Who of the Israelites are to be consistently presumed to have been told that they would enjoy that pretended glorious future? Surely, not the wicked part. For they, as the prophet foreshows in his denunciation, would fall a prey to the sword of the invaders. It was only the just that would be spared and survive (ch. III. 10). They were the "remnant" assigned for salvation, and they with their posterity would be deemed worthy of the restoration of the tutelary relations between Jehovah and Israel (ch. IV. 2-6). Now while, in the rigid view of condign Divine recompense as maintained in many parts of Scripture,[33] it would indeed be quite conceivable to attribute to the prophet the intention of particularizing in favor of the smaller portion of the Judeans—that very "remnant"—and pronouncing them alone as destined to share in the prospective Messianic bliss, we can yet not bring ourselves to ascribe such exclusive meaning to the tenor of that brilliant forecast. Its tone is altogether too general and generous for that. There is, considering the paragraph in itself, such a genuinely and broadly national scope impressed on it, that to impute to it any partiality for the righteous and pious minority of Israel would be almost preposterous. But yet, when we view it logically and in the context of the whole range of denunciations contained in the before-noted sequel, there is nothing left for us but to infer that the prophet meant really to declare the large, part of Israel shut out from the prospective realm of bliss.

Yet our question must assume a still more striking force under the following aspect. Can we hold it for one moment consistent with the national self-consciousness or lofty patriotic pride of the prophet, to have particularized in that brilliant forecast in favor of the just "remnant" of Israel, when we notice him at the same time to have foretold that "all the nations" would at that glorious eventuality be drawn to the illustrious centre of peace-inspiring theocracy, Jerusalem? (See ch. II. 2-4). Must his national pride not have forbidden him to so discriminate against the general body of his own people as to assign the enjoyment of the future blissful era to a just and pious remainder only? We can indeed well conceive and reconcile in our mind that an Israelitish prophet would adjudge to converted pagans an equality of spiritual advantage with his own nation. This is even illustrated in Isa. LVI. 1-8. Yet it exceeds our comprehension that a national Israelitish preacher should have meant to award to pagan converts a superiority of divine favor above any part of Israel, however grievous their backsliding and defection from their God, and however severe he had otherwise to be in his animadversion of their wrongs. No, such insinuation must, on general principles, be repulsed. This repulsion is, in very fact, fully supported by the view above noted, that the tone of that peace paragraph is alike too general and generous to allow of its discriminating limitation to a just "remnant." But yet, on the other hand, this limitation would be glaringly established in view of the logical and contextual conclusion also above noticed.

How then, let us ask, must those luring phrases of a coming golden era of peace at the head of Isa. ch. II. impress us? Surely, as inconsistent, not only with the whole context but also with itself—if the premise of the exclusion of the majority of ill-deserted Israel from the realm of bliss holds, as it logically and contextually must.

This positive contextual inconsistency would even

practically tempt, nay prompt us to assume, as the inevitable upshot of our questioning, that Isaiah's famous peace paragraph came by its present position through some literary or editorial mischance. Isaiah, we readily concede, may have adopted it from an older source for use at some public oration. But, we have to say emphatically on the other hand, he could certainly not have spoken it in the same strain with the previous and subsequent context, which is so utterly contrary to it in texture and tendency. Even if it were supposable that he spoke it nevertheless in the connection in which it is found, because the signature of "latter day" is attached to it which renders the prediction but as eventual, yet this at least cannot reasonably be gainsaid that the sharp contrast of that actual juxtaposition must have sorely jarred the ears and feelings of his hearers. This contrast must necessarily have made of no avail the whole soothing and uplifting purpose he might have associated with it in his mind. Unless, therefore, we could suspect that the prophet was of such a careless temper as to jump in a breath from the one extreme of glowing promise of bliss to the other of terrible and stunning denunciation of divine vengeance, or that he was so unconcerned about the order of his own writings as that in collecting them he took no heed at all of their logical consecution, we have to account for that strangest of all juxtapositions by assigning it not to the prophet himself, but to a later transcriber or editor.[34] Such a one, in the simple piety and regard for the extant compositions of the great and renowned prophet, Isaiah, would subordinate every sensible concern for consistency to the reverent motive of preserving intact every

Presages of a Coming Golden Era of Peace. 45

sentence and word accredited to the prophet, for the hereditary sacred possession of Israel. Thus it may have come that he placed the questionable peace paragraph where it now stands, indifferent to the simple requirement of logical arrangement and consecution, and indifferent, also, to the future charge, by more critical readers, of his most uncritical proceeding.

This seems the only alternative by which we could reduce and mitigate the objections, which stand out against that celebrated Isaianic passage of brightest national hope for the future.[35]

Let us now consider the almost identical Messianic peace predictions in the prophet Micah, ch. IV. 1-4. It will disclose to us the same enormous incongruity of context. We invite attention to the contrast of chapter III. with IV. 1-4. In the former place the prophet had put forth the most scathing reproof of his countrymen for their various iniquity. In the last verse, 12, he denounced in punishment of it the most direful and startling national calamity: "Therefore shall Zion for your sake be plowed as a field, and Jerusalem shall become heaps (viz., of debris), and the mountain of the house as the high places of the forest." The denunciation must have made an uncommonly striking and wounding impression, judging from the reference to it in Jeremiah XXVI. 18 sq. The threat that the wickedness of the Judeans had brought on them an impending doom of the total destruction and annihilation of Jerusalem with its temple, was indeed not accomplished. Its non-accomplishment is Providentially accounted for in Jeremiah l. c. ver. 19. But this does not immediately concern us here. What we have to urge, and urge as most vexatious and utterly incomprehensible is, that immediately upon that fatal threat the prophet bursts suddenly forth into the other extreme of the golden vision of an elysian future. In this glowing picture Jerusalem with its temple, the abode of Jehovah, passes as flourishingly existent, and towards this sanctuary there is, as the presage there reads, to be attracted the whole world to draw from it instruction for guidance and conduct; also, peace would be universal, and Israel enjoy blessed security—the very consummation of peace in their traditional conception of the corresponding Hebrew term. There occurs in the whole paragraph not the least intimation that the "latter days'" blissful condition would be of a kind that might be construed as compatible with that paralyzing close of chapter III., namely, that it would ensue after the catastrophe denounced here. The prophet strikes in those initial lines of ch. IV. the most serene notes of bright hopefulness, as though that last sentence of the preceding chapter with its dire forecast had not been written or uttered at all. Is this not a most irreconcilable contrast? There are certainly no sharper opposites than penal ruin and glorious happiness. Yet these are placed in Micah's prophecies close upon each other! That a line of capitular division separates them in form, does not in the least alter the flagrant contradiction of both those utterances. It matters nothing that they are separated by such outward marks, as long as they are proved or supposed to come from the same author who apparently gave both of them forth in all earnest. If he did at both times mean what he said—and we have certainly no right to suspect that he was trifling with the good sense and good faith of his hearers or readers—we must at least charge him with the most faulty memory, which would not serve him even beyond the vanished breath of a directly preceding sentence, into the immediately following one of another chapter. Yet as this, again, would be too curious a psychological phenomenon to be seriously entertained, we have to try to lift the difficulty of their irreconcilable contrast in the same manner we did with the difficulty offered by the kindred peace paragraph of Isaiah: that is, we have to declare Micah's peace prediction, too, out of place in the context in which it is found, and attribute its fixed incorporation to a redactor who proceeded thoughtlessly in arranging the remaining literary productions of the prophet.

The latter had doubtless, like his contemporary, Isaiah, appropriated and assimilated in his fond soul that glowing picture of futurity which had come down from an anterior period. And he, like this contemporary, had unquestionably cherished it for some oratorical purpose of captivating the ears of his hearers, which he would accomplish at a time when they would be deserving of a bright outlook being held out to them. But never, we aver, could either prophet have uttered that peace paragraph before the people, when he was in the excited mood of indignation, which prompted him to hurl at their conscience grave charges and bitter denunciations, such as are found in the last verse of chapter III. of Micah, or in the orations of Isaiah from chapter II. to IV.

Nor could such brilliant peace predictions ever have counterbalanced the hard and heavy realities of unrest, tumult and struggle with which the life of the nation of Israel was beset in those ancient prophetic times. They were, strictly viewed, no more than thin gossamers floating in the air, doing at best the momentary good of soothing the people's hearts, which smarted alike from oppressive outward conditions and the stings of monitions and rebukes with which the same prophets treated them again and again.

We see, then, how frail the mere literal and logical foundation of those almost identical peace paragraphs of Isaiah and Micah is. When we hold yet in mind the irrepressible rational judgment, that all such bright forecasts of bliss and glory were in their nature nothing but a fabric of fancy, sweet at the moment of their conception and utterance, but bitter in the sequence, as the indefinitely long delayed realization must have sorely harassed the hearts of those to whom they were addressed, we have to insist that their merit of temporarily counteracting the popular depression of spirit must have been very precarious indeed. The present evil and the fear of equally hard or still worse impending evil was, we have to judge, too heavy a weight on their minds to allow them to be carried away with the prophets' own actual or ostensible enthusiasm.* And it is this circumstance, too, that forbids us rating those peace predictions too high, or resorting to them in any serious manner, and especially attaching to them any dogmatic importance for those times or any other time.

Dogmatism, that is, the positive religious-like assumption based on those prophetic messages, that a

---
*See Excursus.

Presages of a Coming Golden Era of Peace. 49

Messianic peace reign to come was or is part of God's providential design for the farther future, must, on the whole, recede with abashment before the stern fact of their becoming meaningless by the mere contextual relations in which they stand in either Isaiah or Micah. Nor will any rational reader contend that a prophet could, because of his exalted state of mind, have also exalted himself above the ordinary prerequisite of straight logic. A prophet, like Micah, for instance, no more than any other human being, could sensibly defy the cogent argument that the denunciation of ch. III. 12, and the promise of IV. 1-4, are irreconcilable opposites, mutually exclusive and never tractable enough to be made to join hands. Only one of those opposite propositions could be thought as real or capable of being realized.

Close and critical examination, then, brings out clearly and irrefutably the circumstance, that those Messianic peace forecasts not only partake of the suspended nature of any promise resting on no foundation presently justifying it, but show, besides, a glaring unreality in the very contexts in which they appear.

Still more striking instances of the problematic character and suspense adherent to those peace presages for nearer or farther-off times, we have to produce. We shall now deal with direct announcements of an expected personal (Messianic) ruler. By the way of anticipation we will state at once as the result of this inquiry, that the concept of prosperous futurity to be construed from them can be none other than 'through bloody war to sweet Messianic peace.'

We will refer first to Micah ch. V. The feature of the golden age to come, in which all nations would quit warring and peace would universally dominate, so charmingly presented in ch. IV. 3, receives additional exultant illustration in the promise of the rise of an illustrious king in that next chapter. Of this predicted ideal monarch we have already treated above. He is portrayed as of egregious sway and as the very incarnation of peace in the intense and extensive meaning of the equivalent Hebrew word "shalom," especially as to its combined implication of abiding national and individual happiness. But this, we must say, is only a glaring veneer covering over stark realities and gloomy conditions, for a momentary end of captivating and soothing the hearers. That lustrous "consummation devoutly to be wished" must to the practical and cool observer of the political complexion of the Jewish State as it then was, have seemed far and possibly farther distant than ever before.

The prophet himself who painted that brilliant picture of futurity could not suppress the jarring strokes of exceeding difficulty to be overcome antecedently to that happy eventuality. These were, that the potent future peace-king would have plenty of bloody work to do to beat back and defeat hostile invaders. The possibility, in particular, of new warlike attempts upon the Jewish land by the much dreaded, all-conquering great-power, Assyria, with her "army which was always on a war footing" (so Maspero, 'Struggles of the Nations', p. 620), looms up fatally from the background. The apprehension of a new Assyrian invasion, advanced in ch. V. verses 4, 5, puts a strongly disilluding damper upon the whole bright and fascinating Messianic vision. All the God-given greatness and power of the prospective Messiah did not preclude, even in the prophet's own exalted mind and speech, such fatal chances overhanging the nation's horizon. In fact, the golden state of final disarmament of Israel, so gracefully depicted in ch. V. vv. 9, 10, could, by the prophet's own implied admission, not be realized until previously, with *lion-like* force and ferocity, the overpowering hand of Israel would have subdued and destroyed all their enemies (see vv. 7, 8), and this with the miraculous aid of Jehovah, as the Hebrew word "yikkarethu" used in v. 9, seems to indicate .

This shows conclusively enough that neither was the outlook at the time of those prophetic utterances propitious enough for a realization of the glorious Messianic peace-empire, nor could the prophet himself in his clear and collected thought have consistently conceived of any realization of it, before the manifold oppressive and ruinous power of Israel's foes was entirely undone. What stupendous and heroic warlike measures and enterprises would be required to accomplish this end, no sensible prophet of the eighth century B. C., which was so very calamitous for all Israel, could have concealed in his own mind. Neither a Zechariah, nor an Isaiah, nor a Micah, who were contemporary witnesses of that convulsive period in Israel's history, could reasonably shut his eyes to the fierce menace to which the Jewish land was then incessantly exposed. If they nevertheless came before the people with their bright promises of a marvelously happy and glorious future, they acted mainly, as already repeatedly suggested, from a motive of sympathy with their downcast and despairing compatriots, stimulating their courage to bear up under the visitations and steeling them for as much resistance as they could muster.

They were also, doubtless, themselves enthusiasts, bred and imbued with the then already traditionary notion of a halcyon era to come to Israel, which lifted their own minds above the stress and distress of the actual wretched conditions of the nation. The first bright ray of light and relief from foreign oppression, the first calm, untroubled hours after a long and hard tumult of national anxiety, were enough to stir their own hearts again with the high national hopes of the past. Fancy would then promptly step in, "flinging for them an airy bridge" across the present chasm, and throwing its connecting spans out and back into the reign of David, the palmy days of which passed in tradition as excelling in true prosperity any other period in the national history. What was, they would imagine, could, under God, be again. Jehovah might let rise again a mighty and illustrious Davidide, who would marvelously fill the present chasm with his and the nation's power and glory. It is, there is good reason to suppose, in those temporary lulls of foreign menace or aggression that there may be discovered the origin of most, if not all the gorgeous predictions of peace, security, splendor and might, which came from their high-flown minds and inflated lips. We will make this view most plausible by a reference to the very significant and notorious prophecies written or delivered immediately or soon after king Hezekiah's accession. This we attempt to do in the separate Excur-

Presages of a Coming Golden Era of Peace. 53

sus. Here we aim to further show with convincing force that the predictions of a coming glorious peace era uttered by the prophets of the Assyrian epoch, could mean only, if they were to mean anything at all, the attainment of peace, after wading first through vast streams of blood shed in terribly destructive warfare.

Let us look at the remarkable passage of Isaiah XI. 1-10. It is like the previously noted one of Micah, a typical Messianic forecast. And it is, too, of the same type with it in the prediction of a God-endowed Davidic ruler to come (compare Micah V. 3 with Isa. XI. 2), only more elaborate in the description of his qualities and the blessed efficiency of his dominion. That it is organically connected with ch. IX. 5, 7, is to us open to no question. This point of view we have marked already above (note 21). It deserves, indeed, an ever newly reiterated assertion, in the face of the apparently never ending mysticism in which it is, in some of its parts at least, so persistently folded up for the purpose of a one-sided dogmatic scheme.

The oracle of ch. XI sets off the coming ruler's chief trait of character as that of consummate righteousness—the basal condition, indeed, of any government's peaceful and prosperous progress.[36] Profound peace will prevail under him (compare also IX, 5, 6), both by his own disposition and the dispensation of Jehovah, who will cause even the noxious beasts to lose their ferocious bent and become tame and mild towards the rest of the animals (verses 6-8).[37] He will be the central banner towards which all peoples will tend in homage and adoration: thus eminent and illustrious will be the coming Jerusalemite Messiah and world-ruler.

Yet soon the prophet tones down again his overdrawn strains of promise. As though he had suddenly awaked from a teasing and abortive dream, he reflects again upon the sordid and sorrowful realities and dangers that actually subsisted, contravening the brilliant outlook he had so blandishingly held out to his hearers. As though the previous happy prediction had not at all been made, he reasons again in an anxious and warlike tone. His grandiose oracle having spent its dazzling sparkles, he falls back again upon the actual dreary present with its various perils threatening the nation.

When he in the sequel, vv. 11-13, predicts a re-gathering of all the exiled Israelites from the four ends of the earth,[38] to be firmly cemented together again as one, undivided nation, and thus unitedly to enjoy the blissful government of the God-endowed Anointed, we are fain to expect the illustration drawn out subsequently, that then all those returned and brotherly confederate masses of Israel would have to do nothing but indulge the sweet consciousness of re-acquired national bliss, and, in the proud feeling of themselves, look on self-complacently how other nationalities would come and offer allegiance to their Anointed and approach them, the newly elevated, great and commanding nation, in a submissive attitude, cravingly suppliantly their favor and good-will. But no; this would not ensue. At any rate, the prophet has not opened such perspective. What he practically indicates is, that the Messianic-theocratically united Israel would then stand shoulder to shoulder—to engage in

Presages of a Coming Golden Era of Peace.

the bloody business of war. The previously pictured universal peace was therefore but an airy hypothesis. It meant at best, as to Israel, an armed peace—such as European nations present yet in our day—a peace resting on and combined with the alleged illimitable and insuperable power of the Messianic king, (compare IX. 6). By this combination would, on the one hand, Israel's enemies be held in awful check and, on the other, Israel themselves be enabled to take dire vengeance on and make bloody conquest of the various Palestinian nationalities, who were of an ever hostile temperament and attitude against them. If the Israelitish hearer or reader of those sweet delineations of promise, in vv. 1-10, was rocked into the happy dream that with the arrival of the ideal ruler all would be peace and rest, he was suddenly shaken out of it again by the picture of the stern eventuality of having to reduce by warlike enterprises the different hateful neighboring nationalities. Surely, Israel under those imagined ideal conditions would easily be able to cope with them. Yet the prospect of bloody warfare can never leave any, even the most powerful nation, in a calm and unruffled mood of mind.

The prophet holds out that those rejoined masses of Israel would under the leadership of their august Messianic monarch "fly upon the shoulders of the Philistines, spoil all the children of the east, lay their hand upon Edom and Moab, and the children of Ammon shall be reduced to dependence" (v. 14).[39] Even the miraculously striking "rod of mouth and breath of lip" of the Messiah will not suffice to subdue and conquer those nationalities. He will not only be "girded with rightcousness," but will have eventually to gird on his real sword and don the rest of his steel armor, to lead on his Israelitish troops in bloody assaults upon these nationalities—a fierce warrior, again, instead of a gentle peace ruler. How can this latter statement, we ask, be made to accord with the previous lines, also with ch. IX. 6, and especially with ch. II. 1-4, predictive of universal peace?

Delitzsch, too, in his commentary in loco, makes the same kind of observation. He says: "But how does this warlike outlook tally with the preceding promise of a paradisean peace, which presupposes an entire cessation of war, as foreshadowed in Isa. ch. II. 4? It is a contradiction which can be solved only from the point of view that the contents of ver. 14 are only images taken from the warlike present, but typifying the future dominion of united Israel over the neighboring nations by means of spiritual weapons." Now, we contend against that most learned exegetist, this shift of declaring as typical what cannot stand the test as a real and literal representation, meets in the present days of rational and critical interpretation of Scripture certainly with but few adherents. We at any rate repel as the most daring venture and dubious dealing with old sacred texts, any such attempt at symbolizing relative expressions in instances which show on their face and from all internal reasons that they can bear a literal meaning only. We freely admit that the old prophets used at times, and at times rather prominently, a figurative language. But, we hold, there are but few cases in which the intention of the respective writer can, to a scholar versed in

Presages of a Coming Golden Era of Peace. 57

the whole Bible, remain doubtful. He will generally almost unfailingly be able to make out from the tenor and drift of the composition, whether the writer thought to convey a literal or figurative sense. In the case in point we would vouch for and stake our reputation for knowledge on the proposition, that Isaiah never meant there aught but to advance to his Israelitish hearers the relieving prospect, that in the times of Messiah those hateful neighboring nationalities would be coped with in regular warlike fashion, with bow and spear and other material weapons of destruction, should they further undertake, as they so often did before, to molest and make havoc among Israel. The terms used in ver. 14 are those of actual warlike assaults upon insidious Palestinian foes, and nothing else. Nor has the prophet intimated with one word or in any manner imaginable, that in the blessed farther future the people of Israel would handle "spiritual weapons." The Messianic king himself is, truly, pictured as spiritually gifted, and to an almost supernal degree. But as to the mass of Israel we can find no trace in the whole context of that passage that the prophet wished to foreshadow them, too, as thus gifted, so that they might, as Delitzsch would have it, smite the pagan Palestinians with their superior spiritual weapons. Not that it is foreign to an old prophet to predict the eschatological spectacle of intense, even supernatural enlightenment among the multitude of Israel. No, such an instance is really offered in the prophet Joel (ch. III. 1 sq). Even passages like Isa. LIX. 21, may allow of such an over-wrought construction (Ibn Ezra at least puts such construction upon the last-cited passage). But this cannot offset the real textual and contextual sense of the prophecy in point. Here material weapons only could be meant. The Philistines and Edomites, Israel's archenemies, would care very little for the eventuality of the Israelites possessing a high spirit, even a prophetical temper. They would continue to defy the spirit, and mock at the supposed prophets, as they were wont to do formerly, and inflict all possible mischief upon Israel in the future as they did in the past, unless a miracle should prevent their doing so. By a miracle, indeed, Jehovah could curb and restrain the violence aimed by those foes at his people. But then the miracle would be directly God's and not his people's.

We, for our part, can find a solution of that contradiction—and one for which we claim by no means any merit of indisputability—only in either of the two following suppositions. We may uphold the theory of Fürst, mentioned above, that the first ten verses of Isaiah XI. were also, like ch. IX. 1-6, borrowed from an older prophet. Isaiah may accordingly be supposed to have incorporated those verses here to make up an oration for a certain purpose. And it may have been, further, that in the process of welding the matter together, the logical gap thus created was simply blurred over. Or the contradiction may be solved in this manner, and agreeably with our position, that none of those bland and sweet Messianic presages of the prophets are to be taken strictly in their literal import. They were substantially no more than flashes of poetic fancy, flashes focused and conserved that they might occasionally irradiate and solace downcast hearts, and therefore

Presages of a Coming Golden Era of Peace. 59

never to be judged of according to standards of truth or religion; or, if they came from the somewhat convinced hearts of the prophets and were to pass in a literal sense, they could certainly have implied nothing but that the ultimate era which was to dawn and break for Israel would be achieved only after having first disposed summarily of all hostile nationalities from whom attacks were constantly feared.

This view is best instanced by the above-quoted passage of Micah ch. V. 7-10, which may really be regarded as a foremost illustrative specimen marking out the intrinsic merit of all other kindred prophetic utterances as well. In that passage the real and enduring peace-footing of the nation of Israel is manifestly enough prefigured as to take place no earlier than the time when they would utterly have vanquished and prostrated their various, ever menacing foes. This time, freely we say it, never came, and never could come, considering the unfortunate geographical and numerical conditions in which Providence placed that nation.

We see, then, that Isaiah, too, cannot be understood but as conceiving the fond traditionary notion of a future golden era of peace, to be other than the issue of an all around subjugating, sanguinary warfare against those peoples who were and would be ever ready to break in turbulently upon the even course of Israel's calm and prosperous state. This would be virtually equal to the proposition—impossible almost of expression—*through incessant war to lasting peace*. This being so, abiding peace could not possibly be predicted in all earnestness and according to facts which universal human history supplies. Every day might bring to Israel new complications and disturbances. How, then, could such blissful consummation be presaged in advance, and in particular for the whole length of the future time of the princes of the Davidic line, which was to re-open again with the 'Messiah' and be perpetuated in the unbroken succession of these illustrious rulers? Again, could any prophet know beforehand even so much as that the Messiah's own presumptive heir and successor would be held worthy enough in the sight of God to really follow his father on the throne and body forth the theocratic idea and cause in the imagined Jerusalemite center of the divine vicegerency? The prophets, as it seems to result from different Scriptural indications, truly flattered themselves with such fond hope. Yet they could, on the other hand, nowise be certain about its accomplishment, nor be warranted in speaking of it in positive tones of necessary fulfillment. Unless it could be imagined that any one prophet held the curious, vain notion that the hoped-for Messiah was immortal[40] and would reign for ever, we have to declare that none of them was able to predict lasting peace and prosperity for Israel in the supposed Messianic era to come. For while the illustrious coming shepherd of Israel might indeed succeed in establishing an exemplary government of surpassing justice, and signal, enviable happiness among the nation, there was yet no guaranty that this blessed state would unbrokenly endure even under him, much less that it would safely and unfailingly attend all the coming governments of his Messianic successors.

    Now we must not be too critical on points like these.

Presages of a Coming Golden Era of Peace. 61

We ought to, and we readily do, allow for the prophet's emotional conditions into which we of a late generation, and perhaps too sober habits of mind, can no more put ourselves. Further, those mellow and fascinating peace predictions were, on the one hand, but rehearsals of traditionary notions, and, on the other, designed to relieve and soften the effect of the sharp rebukes which those ancient preachers of Israel were prompted to deal to their people. To offset the smart of their rebukes, the other extreme of picturing their future in most roseate colors, if they should repent and return to the pure service of God and to righteousness, was resorted to. All this was an emotional proceeding merely. It rested not on a condition full of such high promise for the future and justifying the forecast.

Both extremes just noted are strikingly illustrated in the prophet Hosea. He lived in the early part of the eighth century and witnessed the terrible and corrupt state of the northern kingdom, his own native land. He poured out his righteous indignation unsparingly and with scathing threats of utter ruin and desolation of country and people. Yet almost in the same strain which dealt the heaviest blow of reproof to his countrymen, he predicted that, if they would bethink themselves and repent, they would be re-accepted into God's favor, and as a result of it God would make an end of the hurtful beasts, of war and its baneful instruments, and let them live in security— peace, indeed—and the enjoyment of plenty. See Hosea II. 16-25.

There is certainly no cogent conclusion from such extravagant orations that the prophets themselves believed religiously in the advent of a golden future of peace, much as they had themselves imbibed the tradition of its expected coming and doubtless indulged, from a patriotic and sympathetic feeling, such expectation with all the rest of the people. At best, the promises of such glorious consummation rested but on emotional grounds. They were not substantial enough to be accounted as involving the probability of realization. Unfortunate realities might at any coming moment belie the promise and thwart the realization. However this may be, and in what manner soever we may judge of the prophetic predictions of an ulterior or ultimate era of peace, this much can never be disputed, that they could not mean aught but to point to an eventuality ensuing after intense and immense warlike struggles. This results incontestably from internal evidences, laid open by a clear investigation of the respective prophetic texts and contexts.

And this was, too, let us add in conclusion, the interpretation which later apocalyptic and apocryphal Messianic writers put on those predictions. One of those writers, upon whom the spirit of the old prophecies seems to have been breathed most genuinely and freshly, the author of the apocryphal Psalms of Solomon, composed after Pompey's conquest of Judea, about the middle of the first century B. C., reasons in this strain. The expected "Messiah, the son of David," will enter upon his dominion of power, peace and prosperity, after having destroyed the heathen invaders of Jerusalem (and the Jewish land) and smitten Israel's foes with the awe of his dread sway, so that they would no more attempt any hostility against his nation (Ps. XVII).

Presages of a Coming Golden Era of Peace. 63

He will indeed not be a warlike ruler (ibid. ver. 37). His true force will consist in his implicit trust in almighty God, who is ever able to keep Israel's enemies in check, if he choose to do so. Yet for all that, the "iron scepter" cannot be spared wherewith he would cast down and "shatter" Israel's foes (ver. 26). Their forcible reduction, in order to render them permanently innocuous, is here necessarily presumed. Truly, again, that Psalmist holds firmly, though not expressly, to the expectation that war will, with the strong establishment of the Messiah's empire, cease forever. Yet in order that such high end of stable peace and security be attained, previous sweeping martial enterprises are indispensable—as we have to judge from the whole tenor of the psalm to have been the writer's supposition. It is only when the Messiah will practically be possessed of almightiness, that he will overawe and terrorize the enemies of Israel with the "word of his mouth" (vv. 27, 39; and this doubtless in accommodation to Isa. XI. 4).

The Sibylline Oracles, too, holding out an era of peaceful and prosperous universal theocracy to be, cannot get away from the notion that war is to precede that blessed ultimate state. In the famous passage, III. 652 sq., the prospective saintly and heroic lord is said to "make the whole earth cease from evil war, killing some and accomplishing faithful covenants to others." This shows conclusively that even this writer of glowing promise for the future could not perceive the golden era of universal peace and good-will under the Zionite theocracy as other than preceded by the violence of destructive war. Nay, even further onsets against the

Jewish land are, despite the presumption of a coming theocratic peace government, anticipated there (see 663-697). God, it is foretold, will deal with those furious enemies of Israel by "war and the sword," amidst other ruinous physical catastrophes. It is only afterwards that "the children of God will live in rest and peace, the hand of the Holy One protecting them" (698-709): even the era of universal peace will then have begun (743-760).

NOTES.

(1). We aim to make it clear by the following reference to the gospel account of Jesus' triumphal entry into Jerusalem. That the multitude acclaiming Jesus on that occasion should have shouted before him "Hosanna," and also "Blessed is he that cometh in the name of the Lord" (Matt. XXI. 9), is in itself indeed credible enough. The latter sentence is extracted from Ps. CXVIII. 26, in which verse it constitutes a clause. The former expression is readily discerned to have also been taken from that context, viz., v. 25. Yet, we have to say, it does not occur there in such apocopate and contracted form. There is, moreover, no Scriptural evidence that even in its longer structure it ever served as aught but an invocation of the Deity. (Alford, in loco, observes that "Hosanna" was "a formula originally of supplication, but conventionally of gratulation." But he fails to quote any external source from which he could have derived the latter assertion. For aught we know, it would be most difficult, nay impossible to bring such support). But for all that we hold it possible that it was already in the days of Jesus vulgarly employed in that shorter form in which we see it practically used in the account of Jesus' triumphal entry. We know that the medieval Rabbinism adopted "hoshana" as a technical designation of the ritualistic willows of the seventh day of the Feast of Tabernacles, and even as a particular name of this day itself, which was the "great hoshana." It is therefore not unreasonable to suppose that that popular contraction of the phrase had already been accomplished in Jesus' time, and been used freely for the same ceremonial denotations. From the use in connection with ceremonial objects it may have been extended, too, as an expression of acclaim and homage, in the manner in which it appears also in the gospels. Yet for all that we have to declare it utterly inconceivable that the same multitude, consisting doubtless mostly of unlearned folk, should have newly coined, and on the spur of the moment, the additional phrase, "Hosanna in the highest," which is also put into their mouth in the above-noted gospel. There was, we assert, no analogy for it anywhere in Hebrew Scripture. No celestial anthem is in its entire volume represented under such form. We have therefore no alternative but to assume that the gospel writer created it anew from his own mind, accomplishing it by way of discursive reference to the cited psalm verse. In Luke the case is still more aggravated. He enlarges the acclaim, "Blessed, etc.," by inserting "king"—a new formation again—and attributes to the multitude the further exclamation: "peace in heaven and glory in the highest" (XIX. 38). The latter phrase, we remark, is evidently stereotyped with Luke, as would appear from the parallel of ch. II. 14, which is the subject proper of our disquisition. The phrase is, truly, fitting enough, though it is not borne out by any direct and exact Hebrew Scriptural analogy. As we have set forth elsewhere in our text, it is likely to have been substantially drawn from Ps. CXLVIII. 1. Yet, we have curiously to ask, how did Luke come to combine with it the other phrase, "peace in heaven?" We cannot possibly detect in it any intelligible import, and certainly no sense appropriate to the occasion. It may be accounted for, though, as a random formation from Job XXV. 2. This passage may have been present to Luke's mind when he put down that account. But then we have to conclude that he thought fit to utilize it in his own way, without stopping to reflect upon the organic meaning it has in that context of Job, a meaning entirely inapplicable, in fact, to the event of Jesus' entry. Moreover, the phrase as produced by Luke is liable to be understood as an imputation that God had until then lacked peace, which was now fairly assured and firmly established for evermore. If it be said that this is not a necessary deduction from Luke's phrase, we reply, that we marvel what other reasonable construction could at all be placed on it.

(2). Such as Bleek, Olshausen, Ewald, Tischendorf, etc. The last-named defends it on the ground, that the "hymn is most fitly divided into two clauses, of which the first reaches to "Theo," and the other contains the rest." We, for our part, have to own that we fail to see wherein that fitness should subsist. It can be made out the less, when we bear in mind that the amalgamation of all that ensues upon "Theo" into one clause, requires the construction of the genitive, "eudokias." This construction, however, gives in our opinion no tolerable sense. Our objections to it are set forth at length in the text of our essay. Let us yet note, that Keim, to us the foremost and most competent of all the writers of the Life of Jesus, accepts also the reading "eudokias," in the genitive. "Otherwise," he observes, "there are three members in the sentence, only one for God, two for man, and these moreover opposed to each other without real antithesis."

Here we deem it in place to present that eminent scholar's observations on the entire respective passage of Luke. Contrasting (in 'The History of Jesus of Nazara', II. 79 ff.) Matthew's brief notice of the birth of Jesus, he says of Luke: "Luke and his Ebionite authority have provided more extensive scenery for the birth itself—signs in heaven and on earth, etc. . . . Luke's Ebionite informant has to tell of blinding glory from heaven, of a watch both human and angelic which welcomes the new comer with warmth and solemnity combined. An angel of the Lord appears (here he remarks in a note: "Luke is elsewhere full of ideal allusions"). In Bethlehem he arouses none from slumber it is true; but he makes his way to the shepherds, ... and declares to them instead of fear, great joy for the whole people, "for unto you is born this day, etc." And while he names to them the sure sign (v. 12), a heavenly host surrounds him rejoicing in the deed of God, congratulating these representatives of humanity on the gracious advent, "Glory be to God in the heights and welfare upon earth to men in whom he is well pleased." The heavens retired from view, the shepherds hastened, sought and saw the child, etc."

In this connection it may not be amiss to bring forward Strauss' relative judgment. In 'Life of Jesus' (4th ed., transl. by George Eliot) he dilates first on Luke's chronological incongruities (as to the census, etc.),

Presages of a Coming Golden Era of Peace. 69

and on his design to "accommodate the time and circumstances attending the birth of Jesus to his pleasure." He produces then the various constructions put on those circumstances by different expositors. First he mentions the supranaturalistic construction, then the attempt at a natural explanation, and lastly he gives his own interpretation. This is, that the whole narrative of Luke's is entirely mythical. He advances: "The mythi of the ancient world more generally ascribed divine apparitions to countrymen and shepherds; the sons of the gods and of great men were frequently brought up among shepherds." (He might have cited as parallel also the legendary circumstances attending the birth of Buddha.) He insists, conclusively, that "historical truth is not to be sought either in chapter II. or I. of Luke."

(3). Before arriving at this final decision he had entered into Lange's own construction of the sentence, concurring in it in the main, not only in regard to the reading "eudokia," in the nominative, but also as to his assumption that the "theme and motive" of the whole angelic song was to be sought in that very word. He could only not subscribe to Lange's interpretation of "eirene" as "praise and honor." According to this German commentator the sense of the doxology would be: "Glory to God in the highest, and on earth praise, (because there is) good-will (of God) towards men," namely, through the reconciling power of the (eventual) death of Jesus, then come into being.

(4). Bloomfield, in his commentary, in loco, gives implicitly the same dogmatic turn to the doxology. He contends though for the received reading "eudokia," also for the grammatical division of the sentence into three members. We infer from his observations the following sense to be put on the doxology: "Glory to God in the highest, (for) on earth (there is) peace (viz., with God), among men (God's) good pleasure." The two last clauses he takes as containing the cause and motive for the doxology proper.

(5). It would seem to us that among the early Christ-believers there was the habit of denoting technically any prophetic Messianic presage, either traditionally regarded as such or newly invested with such ultimate bearing, as "good" or "glad tidings."

It strikes us further as probable, that Christianity itself had originally received as title that favorite expression, the "good tidings (or gospel) of peace." At its very beginning, when it consisted only in the preaching of the approaching Kingdom of God, this preaching itself passed under that attractive name. At the later point, when Paul had advanced his own theological system, it is patent from Rom. X. 15 that he applied, mentally at least, that appellation to Christianity as he had himself construed it.

The phrase, it is deserving of notice, points to Isa. LII. 7, as its source of derivation. While Nahum II. 1, has the same expression "gospelling of peace," yet the stronger probability is that its Christian adoption was from the former place. We base it on the consideration that a certain partiality to the prophecies of the Second Isaiah, alike by Jesus and the early Christological writers, can variously be traced and proved to have been settled in Christianity already at its earliest time. It is especially the local environment of that phrase in Isaiah which was exploited with set purpose and marked fondness for Christian evidences. That the notorious sequel, beginning with Isa. LII. 13, was by Christian Messiahists eagerly seized and treated for doctrinal objects, is easily provable and will by no competent inquirer be called in question. If, then, the votaries of the new creed sought for a suitable name which they might give it, they had not to search long for it. It offered itself promptly from the same chapter with which they were so well familiarized.

We remark additionally that there is all the greater probability that the phrase in point was taken from Isaiah and not from Nahum, when we recollect that Paul, in reflecting on the preaching of the Christian system as the "glad tidings," in Rom. X. 15, 16, quoted the whole verse of Isa. LII. 7 (the final clause excepted), of which that phrase forms a part.

It is yet to be noted, however, that its appropriation with a Messianic meaning was but arbitrary, and had no countenance from the logical sense it bears in the prophetic passage. In neither passage of Isaiah or Nahum, we aver, the "gospelling of peace" can be given out as really or even figuratively referable to Messiah. The Messiah is not mentioned or thought of in either place. It is God himself who is represented as dealing with Israel's foe—Assyria in the one and Babylonia in the other prophet. The announcement of shalom "peace" to Israel was thought by those prophets exclusively as being in consequence of the overthrow of the hostile power by God himself—the Messiah having nothing to do with it.

(6). Repentance and remission are named together as the combined theme of the preaching in the name of

Jesus; see Luke XXIV. 47. The association of both those concepts in the mind of the author of Luke and Acts was so strong and tenacious, that in the latter book Jesus is mentioned, even in his heavenly abode, where he is Prince and Saviour, as "giving to Israel repentance and remission."

(7). See 'Acts' by Zeller, who holds that the greater part of the first two chapters of Luke is of Jewish-Christian origin. He otherwise assumes, however, that the author of the gospel bearing Luke's name was not a Jew.

(8). The summons may fairly be construed as inclusive of that part of the heavenly host which were not present at the scene, and possibly likewise of the celestial bodies generally, just as in the cited psalm, v. 2.

(9). To assert again and again a genuinely and strictly Jewish base for the original Christology is certainly not gratuitous, considering the great diversion from it by a more or less contrary dogmatic maze in which it had been involved soon after the lifetime of Jesus, and in which it rests yet to a preponderant degree. The time is not yet come for a more general free and right historical estimate of the claim and aim of Jesus. But come it will, with the rapidly advancing clear and untrammeled search into all facts of history. We for our part seek to bring out those remarkable and weighty points into full light, in our yet manuscript work, 'The Messiah of the Jews'. We hope to be able to give it to the world next year.

The base we mentioned is the Jewish national. Jesus' consciousness was irrefutably that of a national Jewish Messiah. That it was essentially affected by the (apocalyptic) Enochic exalted notions of Messiahism, which partly altered the traditional and popular Jewish conception of Messiah, is true ; also that Jesus' religio-ethical system, if as such the various respective utterances attributed to him in the records may be fixed, partook largely of the Essenic body of doctrines and precepts, is no less verifiable. Yet for all that must his life, character and claim never be considered away from that national Jewish foundation. It admits of no question that national Messiahism was the keynote of his self-feeling from the earliest time of his known public life, and his prime advent—his birth—could accordingly have been celebrated in the oldest sources only as that of a purely and exclusively Jewish Messiah. The Jewish national element predominates e. g. in Matt. XIX. 28, though it appears here suffused with what we may fitly call the Enochic theory. It came practically and unmistakably forward in the decisive event of his noted entry into Jerusalem (ibid. XXI). And it outlasted his life, as it is most strikingly and convincingly evident from the passage of Acts I. 6, 7.

Let us adduce two great representative and accredited writers of the Life of Jesus who, with a number of other independent and unbiased Christological scholars, look at Jesus' claim as Messiah in about the same light of Jewish national consideration.

Keim (l. c.) in his discussion of the 'Kingdom of Heaven' advances: "All existing evidence goes to prove that his kingdom of heaven was a kingdom on earth." It was only later that he "created for his Messiahship, which was threatened by his death, the new, transcendent, eschatological heavenly support." A "material

Messianic feature" Keim discovers at least "in the initial attitude of Jesus," though he allows for the "spiritual and moral fundamental character of his ministry." But for all that Jesus "never transformed, by so-called advancement, the material idea of the Messiah into a purely spiritual one." He "preached a terrestrial kingdom and taught a Messiah who was to return to his terrestrial kingdom." He did not "repudiate the Messianic expectations of the age," though he gave a different turn to the current "conception of the terrestrial kingdom" of Messiah in its application to his own claim, and "never sought to set up such kingdom himself or by the power of the sword."

Strauss' summary view (l. c.) on the Messianic endeavor of Jesus is as follows: "Thus we conclude that the Messianic hope of Jesus was not political, nor even merely earthly . . . ; as little was it a purely spiritual hope : but it was the national theocratic hope, spiritualized and ennobled by his own peculiar moral and religious views."

(10). In the meaning "prosperity," shalom is frequently paralleled by tobh "good." See Jer. VIII. 15; XIV. 19. Isa. LII. 7. Consistently, we find often the opposite of shalom noted as raah "evil;" see Ps. XXVIII. 3; Isa. XLV. 7.

(11). Compare also "time of grace" (Isa. XLIX. 8) which, as is clear from its parallel "day of salvation," has the same Messianic (or rather redemptive) import. A Christological turn it received already by Jesus, who in his supposably first public self-avowal as Messiah, applied it, together with its preceding context, to his own Messiahdom; see Luke IV. 18. That this account, at any rate so far as Jesus' self-attribution of that context is concerned, is genuine, there can be no doubt. It is fully attested by Matt. XI. 4, 5. It is then, seeing that that Isaianic passage with its shenath ratson "acceptable year," had been fully received and firmly domesticated within the Christian body, not at all strange that Luke should in his gospel, in the doxology, have alluded to that Hebrew term "ratson," rendering it with "eudokia." It will appear the less strange when we further remember that this same writer of Luke-Acts produced in Acts X. 38, the identical application of that passage of Isaiah to Jesus. This proves clearly that this passage was fixed in his thought as a Jesulogical staple reference. We hold it consequently most plausible that the "eudokia" of the doxology was by Luke meant to refer to Isaiah's "year of grace" or "accepted year," which expression had from the earliest days of Christianity been employed as evidence for the truth of Jesus' Messiahdom.

That "eudokia" is not the rendering of that expression in the Septuagint, can be no valid objection. The intrinsic sense at any rate of both the word employed in the latter place and of 'eudokia' is identical, meaning "divine acceptability."

It may not be amiss to remark yet, that with our explanation even the genitive, eudokias, would not conflict, provided it could be made probable that in the transcription or translation from the original record a suitable word, governing eudokia, dropped out accidentally or was designedly eliminated for the sake of conciseness. We could then think of "year," as in Isa.

LXI. 2, or "time," as ib. XLIX. 8, being understood as the governing word.

(12). Sins of Israel prevented the coming of the Messianic redemption—this view predominates in the old Rabbinic literature, as we illustrated in "The Sabbath in History," II. 153 sq. We there endeavored also to make out that John the Baptist's and Jesus' cry of repentance had for motive the same traditional notion.

(13). For the sublime estimate placed in Israel on shalom "security," see Isa. XXVI. 3, and compare Zech. II. 8, 9. Akin to the concept in the latter passage are Jer. XLIX. 31 and Ez. XXXVIII. 11.

(14). The first commentator who suggested this origin was the noted German theological scholar, Hitzig. He based it on some parallelisms with the prophet Joel. His conjecture is that the passage in question which now stands in Isa. II. and Micah IV., had its place originally at the end of Joel's extant oracles. Yet he uttered this supposition of a Joelic origin without any assurance, as he admitted that there were objections against it. Nevertheless, Ewald, in his 'Prophets of the O. T.,' has approved and appropriated it. Fürst too adopted it in his 'Hist. of the Bibl. Lit.' Knobel, and others (cited by Steiner, the more recent editor of Hitzig's Commentary on the Minor Prophets, p. 214) urged the grave objection against it, that such generous universalism as is embodied in that passage runs counter to the express tendency of Joel.

A number of other eminent expositors of both previous and more modern days, while they discountenance a Joelic origin of the passage, hold the general view that

Presages of a Coming Golden Era of Peace. 77

it belongs originally to some unknown prophet older than either Micah or Isaiah.

Cheyne, 'Introduction to the Book of Isaiah,' says that he had formerly embraced Hitzig's hypothesis, but surrendered it since in favor of a post-Exilic date of the passage. He maintains also that Isaiah II. 2-4 is taken from Micah IV. 1 sq. He quotes, further, Kuenen's notion that it was a prophetic fragment of an older contemporary of Isaiah and Micah. (To Kuenen we will later recur). He also mentions Duhm's view which agrees with Kuenen's in the estimate that the passage is an older fragment, only that it is to be assigned to Isaiah himself. The prophet, Duhm presumes, wrote it in his old age, in which he laid down his "highest and most sublime ideas" about the future.

Like Cheyne, Nowack,'The Minor Prophets,' assumes a later origin of the passage than the times of Isaiah and Micah, though he does not ultimately decide on a post-Exilic date. Yet he differs from him on the question of the priority of the verses as between Isaiah and Micah. He disputes the possibility of Isaiah having borrowed them from Micah, on the ground that chapts. II.-IV. of Isaiah can scarcely be set down as of a later date than the reign of Ahaz, while the principal activity of Micah fell admittedly, from rather sure evidence, in the days of Hezekiah. (Both these scholars by the bye seem to have influenced our own Professor Toy ('Judaism and Christianity') to incline even to as late a date of Isa. II. 2-4 as the fifth century B. C.) The determining motive in Nowack's argument (in Micah IV.), which made him fall in with the modern critical theory that the passage is of a later date and was by a later hand wrought in the two places where it now stands, was that part of it which deals with the supposed idea of the conversion of the heathens (Isa. II. 2, 3; Micah IV. 1, 2). Though he allows that the Hebrew literature of the Assyrian epoch offers some analogies for the thought of a peace empire to be established in the Messianic times, yet he claims that no parallel is found in it for the other part which has for its subject the universal conversion of the Gentiles to the religion of Jehovah. He admits that "the root of this idea" occurs otherwise in Isaiah, yet in all passages of this kind, he insists, Judah and Jerusalem are always the center: there is no such broad universalism in them as in the passage at issue.

Now this discrimination of Nowack's is absolutely hanging in the air. As though Jerusalem were not everywhere, where the idea of an ethnical attraction to Jehovah is celebrated, either stated or understood as the center! Moreover, Kuenen has already refuted his hypercritical position, that a universalistic temper was entirely wanting to the writers of the earlier times, and also that the earliest date in which those verses of Isa. II. and Micah IV. can have fallen, was that of the Exile. He controverts this modern exegetical extravaganza with very close arguments in his 'Hist.-Crit. Introd. to the Books of the O. T.,' p. 38. It is, in fact, Stade, its spiritual author, whom he calls to task for it. His argumentation applies of course as well against Nowack who follows in Stade's track, as likewise, let us add, against Cheyne who has joined these critics in his more recent exegesis given in 'Introd. to the Book of Isa.' The last-named expositor avows there a change of view from previous time and maintains now that the passage of promise in those two prophets "is the work of a post-Exilic imitator of the older prophets."

It was, we remark, in the first volume of the Zeitschrift für die alttest. Wiss.' (1881), that Stade urged that novel proposition. A later writer, he suggests, who moved in the mental sphere of the Second Isaiah, may have inserted those verses in both places, in Isaiah and Micah. He marks in objection against an Isaianic or Micaic origin and employment of the verses—and in this objection we too share most earnestly and emphatically; see our third chapter of the present disquisition— that in both places, especially in Micah, there is such a decided clash between them and the other context. He declares it utterly improbable that Micah, judging by Jer. XXVI. 17 ff., should have weakened (rather invalidated) the impression of his prophecy contained in ch. III. 12, by an immediately subsequent prediction of its sheer opposite. He then goes on to say that the verses show no relationship at all with the kind of prophecy that prevailed in the Assyrian epoch. Especially does he point out that the universalistic spirit picturing a "concourse of nations coming to Jerusalem to worship," does not fit in with that anterior period, but comports rather with the prophetic tendency of the Exile, such as meets us in Isa. LXVI. 23 (cp. ibid. LX.) and Zechariah XIV. 16-19 (which last he assigns to the period after Ezekiel, even after the Exile). He also observes that the situation in which Jerusalem is depicted in the verses of promise in Micah, differs so essentially from that apparent in the previous chapters I.-III.; and insists, further, that the sentimental expression in Micah IV. 4, has its direct analogue only in late Scriptural utterances. Accordingly, he concludes, we can set down as the earliest possible date of the composition of those verses, Isa. II. 2-4 and Micah IV. 1-4, the period of the Exile.

Stade developed this theory further in subsequent parts of the 'Zeitschrift.' These were however not readily accessible to us. Kuenen (l. c.) is sponsor for the summary opinion, collected from all of Stade's discussions of that subject, that this exegetical critic holds that "the prophets of the eighth century had in their eyes always one people or certain distinct nations and that, though they bring forward now and then an homage rendered to Jehovah by one or more foreign nations, yet the idea of a conversion of "many nations" or "all nations" (compare Isa. II. 2 with ibid. 3, and Micah IV. 1, 2), was yet foreign to them and the ante-Exilic prophecy generally. Against this hypothesis Kuenen, pronouncing it mildly enough as bordering on the hypercritical, adduces an array of ante-Exilic prophecies in which he claims that that idea of Gentile conversion is more or less clearly embodied. (His claim is by the bye only partly justified; however). He concludes by saying: "Unreservedly we admit that that idea became only general, and as well part of the popular belief, during and after the Exile. But this is no ground for denying that already in the eighth century a single prophet may have elevated himself to it."

We fully agree with him in this judgment and reject as totally unfounded that extravagant notion represented by Stade and Nowack.

But we decidely call in question no less the whole pivotal point upon which the latter rests his argument

Presages of a Coming Golden Era of Peace. 81

for a late date of the verses under discussion. He is disposed to let the question of their date stand or fall with the one problem, whether the early prophets Isaiah and Micah were already advanced enough to forecast a general conversion of the Gentiles to the religion of Jehovah. As he has to negative such possibility, he determines ultimately upon the late composition of the verses.

Now we differ positively on the view that a religious conversion of the heathens was alluded to there. We cannot bring ourselves to detect in that prophetic passage of promise any such purport at all. To find with Cheyne, who also takes the respective sentences of that passage in the sense of conversion, in the "ways" of Jehovah (Isa. II. 3) "the rules of moral and religious conduct," and in the issue of teaching from Zion (ibid.) "the revelation of divine truth," is to us an imputation to the prophet of a mental association for which there is no reasonable support in the construction of the whole passage. Not that a universalistic standpoint, including the spiritual hope of a universal acceptance of the true faith of Jehovah by many or all nations of the world, was foreign to the poet-preachers of the eighth century B. C. By no means. We hold them just as capable of having formed such conception as the prophets of and after the Exile. But we maintain, on the other hand, that the context of the passage at issue does not in the least call for such interpretation. Nay, we would even regard it as violence to put such meaning upon it. Let us state it as our conviction that the two leading themes of that passage, the homage owned and rendered to Jehovah by the other nations in Jerusalem, his sacred abode and Israel's national center, and the general (or universal) reign of peace, were intended to bear on Israel only and redound to their benefit and happiness. Care about the welfare of the heathens was not the motive or one of the motives of holding out such an ideal picture of the future. Much less did the thought of their spiritual well-being enter the mind of the prophet, whoever he was that uttered these sentiments first. What he was concerned about in his Hebrew patriotic mind was not the Gentile conversion to true religion, but their conversion to a pacific attitude to his people, Israel. He may, for aught we know, have felt for them in his heart of hearts and wished them all spiritually safe. But the question in our famous passage of promise was not that of the pagans' religious faith, and for their own salvation. It was the question of peace and welfare for Israel in the future which stood uppermost, nay exclusively, before the prophet's vision on putting forth such glowing outlook. It alone made up the basal character of the entire passage. Words of promise that should come home to the real, innermost feeling of the ancient Israelite must have been fraught with the burden of shalom "peace and welfare" for himself and his nation. All that would conduce to and insure this "shalom" was eagerly and supremely desired: even the pagan nations' recognition of Israel's God, in so far, that is, that they would come and consult His oracles in Jerusalem, the seat of His supreme sovereignty, administered temporally by His Anointed Prince, together with His appointed priests and prophets. That they would to this end and on such occasion also bow down at His shrine and offer worship to Him, was a self-evident

Presages of a Coming Golden Era of Peace. 83

supposition, for local adoration was in all oracular seats of the world part of the consultation. But this did not necessarily involve a consistent and stable turn of mind from polytheism or idolatry to Israel's true faith and worship. Those nations might persist—for all the ordinary Israelite cared substantially—in their respective national creeds and worships, as, for instance, the cured Syrian, Naaman, was frank enough to ask for the privilege of making obeisance to Rimmon by the side of his new faith in Jehovah (2 Kings V. 17, 18). Furthermore, a clenching proof of this our view is supplied by the writer of Micah IV. 1-5 himself. Apart from the modern critical question of the authorship of that discourse, there will unavoidably strike the unsophisticated reader the bare fact, that the writer or editor of those five successive verses never for a moment stumbled over the striking inconsistency—if such there really was, as there must have been according to the conversion theorists—of verse 5 with vv. 1, 2. The sense in which that verse appears is undoubtedly: "let all the other nations *continue* to follow their own gods; we will *for ever* adhere to Jehovah, our God." But, we say, there was no such inconsistency felt in the mind of that exponent of Hebrew sentiment. If the condition would once be such that each Israelite could "sit safe and prosperous under his vine, etc." (v. 4), as he had to fear no more any pagan dependence and hostilities, then the consummation of earthly happiness was reached for him and, for the matter of that, the prophet as well. Those pagans might worship whomever they pleased, if they would only be awed by Israel's God into abstaining from troubling and harming

His people. This interpretation is indeed in our perception compelled by the context of Micah at least. The plain sense is: Jehovah's supreme sovereignty once ostensibly recognized by the continuous concourse of other peoples in Jerusalem for receiving oracular revelations in all their politico-social affairs (this is chiefly, if not wholly, the meaning of "Torah" and of the "word of Jehovah" in Micah IV. 1-3), these peoples would accordingly cease all invasions and assaults upon Israel.

Even the re-conversion of their weapons into agricultural implements held out in this prophecy, had not as ultimate view the universal cessation of warfare—for the benefit of the whole world. We freely allow that the prophet will have been large-hearted enough to wish for universal concord and amity between all the nations of the world. But, we protest, he did not mean to convey such sense here. We, for our part, keep firmly to the leading sense of the whole passage of Micah IV. 1-4—and Micah will after all have to be taken with Gesenius, Hitzig and others, despite a certain chronological objection, as the original source from which the kindred passage in Isaiah was transcribed. This sense we find incontrovertibly indicated in the last of the four verses of the passage. It gives, in our opinion, unmistakably the determining logical point of the three preceding verses, in the words, "And they (the Israelites—as no other nation can, from the peculiar choice of phraseology, have been alluded to here) shall sit every man under his vine and under his fig tree, etc." The aim of the whole prediction for the future was, accordingly, no other than Israel's peace and security. This, the prophet suggested, would be insured by the turning, in the after-days, of bloody weapons into utensils of husbandry. And although he adds immediately, "nation shall not lift up a sword against nation," this cannot have been meant, from the sure, single drift of the entire poetical passage, as the ultimate, or even only dominant view the prophet had in mind in this context, however fondly he may, as aforesaid, have otherwise cherished such ideal consummation upon genuine principles of humanity. The reduction and disuse of arms by the Gentile nations would, surely, prevent their warring with one another—and this would be a high blessing for all of them. But the prophet had not here held such blessing in view. He only thought in the main of that blessing which would redound to Israel through such discarding of military instruments by the Gentile peoples.

It was, we aver, neither the peace of the Gentile peoples for their own happiness nor, surely, their religious conversion that was here the object which the prophet had in view. The Torah "instruction" they would seek in "Zion," was no other than the oracular disclosure as to all their cases and causes of a national anxiety. The express expectation was (ibid. 3), that Jehovah would be, with his terrestrial representatives residing in Jerusalem, the warless arbiter in all their feuds and quarrels, mutual as well as, and pre-eminently so, with Israel. It is thus seen that of the two above-noted themes of the prophetic passage in question, the one holding out enduring peace was paramount, and the other only secondary and subsidiary.

Would we say that the religious element was entirely excluded from this prophecy? By no means. More or less of religious "instruction" would inevitably go along with and be attendant on the relations painted by the prophet. To own fealty to a heavenly over-lord and his mundane substitute, means necessarily to heed their combined commandments and rules, both politico-economical and religio-ethical. Moreover, national and religious considerations were in antiquity never held apart, but were intensely and densely interwoven with one another. But what we wished to urge above all was that the conversion of the heathens was in that passage no dominant and independent thought at all, in the sense in which Stade, Nowack and Cheyne construe it.

It thus results, too, that, if Nowack's reasoning were right that there was no other real exegetical obstacle in the way of assigning the passage in point to a prophet of the Assyrian epoch, than the subject of the conversion of the Gentiles alleged to be contained in it organically and conspicuously, it could stand firm and solid as such early prophetic production. The difficulty would be relieved and the older authorship vindicated.

Let us remark that our own view, presented in the foregoing, is apparently shared by Robertson Smith, in his 'Proph. of Israel,' pp. 289 and 291.

Now to return, in conclusion, to Kuenen and his own construction of Isa. II. 2-4 and Micah IV. 1-4. He maintains that neither prophet can be supposed to have copied from the other. He strongly assumes, too, that the passage in either prophet comes from an older original which is, however, not traceable in the extant literary history of Israel. Its author is unknown. He may have been an older contemporary of Isaiah. Kuenen suggests, further, that while there is a possibility that Isaiah took and incorporated it into his own oracles as an introductory discourse, yet, as there is a clashing of context between it and the sequel, it is improbable that the passage should be attributable to Isaiah, even only as an adoption from a prophetic predecessor. He prefers to think accordingly, that it was inserted by the *compiler* of the subject-matter of Isa. II. ff.

(15). That we marked "I. Zechariah" should in the present day scarcely need an explanation. Yet for those unfamiliar with the advanced theological research we remark, that upon fairly indisputable grounds chapters I. to VIII. of Zechariah have been shown to belong to a different author from those of the rest of the book. Upon this the critical scientific theology of modern times is perfectly agreed. A difference of opinion exists only on the latter portion of the book. Some divide it again into two parts with separate authors, while others ascribe it all to one. The tripartite notion is represented by Hitzig, Ewald, Bleek, Reuss, Duhm and others (see Kuenen, 'Introd. to the Books of the O. T.,' II. p. 387).

Stade has developed an independent theory, according to which all the chapters from IX. to XIV. belong to one author only. He is followed by Wellhausen, Rob. Smith and Cheyne (Kuenen, l. c.) Stade, in an essay on the "Second Zechariah," in 'Zeitschr. für die alttest. Wiss.' (1881), declares the criticism which assigns a pre-Exilic date to chpts. IX.-XIV., erroneous. He assumes that these chapters come from one author. Chpts. IX. and X. he adjudges "in general as post-Ezekielic, and in particular as post-Exilic." Ch. XI. he holds connected in sense with XIII. 7-9. Ch. XII. 1-XIII. 6, form to him one oracle. Ch. XIV. he represents as a doublet of ch. XII. 1-14 and XIII. 1-6. On the whole, he sets down all the chapters from IX. to XIV. as a "post-Exilic product, a book younger even than Joel." (The latter has also by modern critics been given such a late date. Kuenen, l. c., p. 331 ff., decides upon it, relegating the book of Joel even into a period later than the middle of the fifth century B. C.)

(16). We will never be certain about the real geographical boundary the Hebrew writers held in view when they attributed to the ideal king an extent of his sovereignity "to the ends of the earth." It is fair to presume that they actually meant in their heart no farther stretch than the Jewish land had gained under David. Consequently, it may only be due to an extravagance of diction when they mapped out the ideal king's rule and possessions, as our prophet did, to reach "from sea to sea (i. e. not only from the Dead to the Mediterranean Sea, but from the Persian Gulf to the Red Sea), and from the Euphrates (this to be understood as a modification of the preceding clause respecting the eastern boundary) to the ends of the earth." The latter terminus may even not have been intended to convey more than merely the Red Sea, implied already in the previous expression, as the western boundary of the Messianic realm. The reiteration of the identical western boundary in other words, would be easily accountable by the manner of Hebrew parallelism.

(17). We admit that the prophet's expression, "speaking peace to the nations," may fairly be construed in a different sense. Upon the analogy of Psalms

Presages of a Coming Golden Era of Peace. 89

LXXXV. 9, it may mean, that the ideal king would be so pacific in temper and disposition, that he would generously decide upon "peace for (i. e. in behalf and for the benefit of) the nations." The expression would then yield the sense, that he would make it his unshaken policy to leave all other nations alone and undisturbed and involve them in no bloody struggles by any attempt at territorial aggrandizement, or from any other warlike motive. It may even, we suggest additionally, have the bare meaning, that the ideal king would put forth his conciliatory efforts at mediating between contending nations and bringing about mutual arrangements, from his pure love of peace, and without asserting ostensibly his authority for directing such peaceable ends. This view too is admissible. However we may understand the phrase, it is in any case testifying of the ideal king's pacific character. As a congenial counterpart to Zechariah's picture of the future Anointed's pacific rule, we may fitly set down Isa. XLII. 1-4. Whoever that mysterious "servant" whose traits are there depicted may be—Cyrus, Israel, or the representative prophet (the Targum and Matthew conceive of him as the Messiah)—we find his traits largely concurrent with those of Zechariah's prospective royal personage. The "servant" too is marked by a mild and modest temperament. He also speaks forth judgments to the nations and gives instructions to the farthest parts of the world. And when he does exercise these functions, he is inspired by a candor (emeth, in Hebrew) which may be taken to imply at once an equitable and affectionate regard for the welfare of those nations.

(18). Even if the Hebrew word "ani" (v. 9) should here only mean "lowly," this would not detract from the main, pacific, interpretation of the ideal king's character. Both qualities, meekness and peaceableness, are cognate and are most often found joined together in truly humane and gentle natures. If we give the word "ani" the sense of "lowly," we have to take the prophet's words as representing that ideal king so meek in temper that he would from his inmost heart eschew, even disdain the magnificence of high station and wealth displayed, according to old Scriptural criterions (see Jer. XVII. 25), in the use of horses and chariots.

(19). We refer for the proper appreciation of this hyperbole, which was apparently stereotyped with the prophets when they discoursed before the common people on the supremacy of the ideal king to come, to note 16.

(20). Fürst, (l. c. p. 467; cp. ibid. p. 302) repudiates positively the idea of the prophet's reference to Hezekiah. The ground he takes is that the golden era of a universal Theocracy with universal peace had not really come with that king of Judah. But this is, to say the least, a most slender argument. As though every prophetic prediction uttered in moments of mental and emotional exaltation had unfailingly to come true! There would indeed be little difficulty to trace in the prophets many more unfulfilled presages than accomplished ones. But with this problem we are not here concerned. We may refer for an intrepid statement of that fact, at least as far as Isaiah is concerned, to various places in Gesenius' commentary on this prophet. As very instructive and suggestive on this point we have to pronounce Bertheau's excellent essay on 'The O. T. Prediction of Israel's Imperial Glory in their own Land' (in 'Jahrb. for German Theology,' 1859). It yet merits notice here that modern half-conservative theology has, in view of that incontrovertible circumstance, contrived the shift of distinguishing between the intrinsic spiritual truth of a prophecy or its potential truth at the time of its utterance, and its real fulfillment. The latter was not an indispensable requisite, and its apparent failure does not alter the authenticity of the prophecy. What this evasive position pushed to a close conclusion amounts to in effect need not be said.

Fürst regards, further, the picture of the ideal king drawn by Isaiah in ch. XI. as a mere "product of fancy," and assumes that the prophet adopted for his purpose the whole respective sketch from an older oracle, that of Joel, just as he imputes the passage of Isa. II. 2-4 to this prior source.

Of the more recent views on that prophetic prediction Cheyne's may be quoted. There is to him "nothing to indicate that he (Isaiah) thought of Hezekiah, or of any of the children of Hezekiah." He firmly holds that the prophet is alike in ch. IX. and XI. "unrolling a picture of the future" (The Prophecies of Isa., 5th ed., revised).

(21). It may, we believe, be most confidently stated that there is a solid, organic connection between this passage and Isa. XI. 1-10. Robertson Smith ('The Proph. of Isr.,' p. 305) completely identifies them. On p. 309 ibid., he even ranges with them in import the promise of Isa. II. 2-4.

Kuenen (l. c.) declares the passages of Isa. IX. and

XI. as "accordant" with each other (p. 52). In a note (p. 54) he says that, considered by themselves, they appear as coincident in time. It must, however, be remarked that that profound critic adduces in the former place several reasons for the assumption that the contents from ch. X. 5 to XI. 1-9 are, partially at least, spurious. He claims that in their present form they came from the pen of a later revising imitator of the body of those Isaianic prophecies.

Cheyne, too, concedes the harmony between the passages of Isa. IX. and XI. In 'Introd. to the Book of Isa.' he calls ch. XI. 1-9 the "companion passage" of ch. IX. 1-6. In 'The Proph. of Isr.' (as above) he says, "the prophecy of XI. 1-9 supplements the vague predictions in chpts. VII. 14-16; IX. 6-7," foreshowing the Messiah as coming from the family of David.

(22). This declaration formed, according to Keim (l. c.) part of Jesus' last conversation with his disciples, before his final journey to Jerusalem, in the year 35. That writer gives the notion that the "energetic sword sermon," with the sentence, namely, "Think not that I am come to send peace, etc.," was spoken by Jesus more to outline his disciples' position than to define his own. Jesus, he says, wished in that sermon to "equip" them "for their independent future campaign." This construction put on that conversation has the ostensible purpose of mollifying the harshness of Jesus' saying. But we object, it does violence to the direct import of the text. Keim's interpretation is by no means supported by the plain, unequivocal phraseology employed in it. This was, we aver, a reference to and explanation of

Jesus' own public work. While we allow readily, as we must, that the words of that conversation which precede and follow the text in point applied to the disciples, it must on the other hand be consistently owned that the words of this text itself could have been used by Jesus for himself only. Keim's reflections on the motive of that conversation of Jesus, which we will immediately reproduce, hold, indeed, in regard to various other occasions, and also in regard to the utterances made here antecedently and subsequently to the text of the "sword sermon"; but they are ill-applied to this very text itself. He observes: "Jesus is compelled to check again and again the sanguine anticipations of the disciples, who . . . . . are ever inclined to dream of the Davidic kingdom, of a kingdom of peace upon earth, of mere rest, joy and blessing, by reminding them of the approaching struggle, and of those sacrifices which they, his successors, must share."

(23). It is curious to notice the various alterations, in Matthew's quotation of that Isaianic passage, of the original Scripture text. The Septuagint have already some deviations from it. Yet our synoptist leaves the Greek version far behind in his effort at recasting it. This is, be it said in passing, but one out of numerous instances in N. T. writings, in which the transmitted Hebrew texts or their equivalent in the delivered Septuagint have unhesitatingly and arbitrarily been reframed for tendency. Space forbids to enlarge on this matter. We can even not discuss the different attempts made by our synoptist at mending the text in question. One of his changes we will however set out, as it is immediately in point. Instead of "He shall not cry," as the perception of the Hebrew original is also in the Septuagint, he has seen fit to render, "He shall not strive." The purpose which induced him to substitute for the unequivocal Hebrew word that expression from his own mind, was doubtless no other than to bring a pretended authentic confirmation of the principle and aim of his gospel, to find Jesus' pliable temper and utter opposition to all strife typified in Hebrew Scripture.

We are yet to observe that we purposely left out in our text the reference to Matt. XI. 29, "for I am meek and lowly at heart." It was for the reason that we hold this expression open to two objections. The first is, that it strikes us as inexact. Doubtless, we assume, it has been imitated from Isa. LXVI. 2. But we hold it no less unquestionable, that in the process of formation after this Isaianic model it underwent a peculiar alteration and transposition. The phrase in Matthew differs from the Septuagint (in loco), in that tapeinos "lowly" is drawn to "heart," while in the Greek version, corresponding to the Hebrew text, it stands alone and the word expressive of the Hebrew "necheh ruach" (Isa. ib.) is "hesychios," which does not occur in the gospel at all. The Hebrew "necheh ruach" denotes there either "downcast," viz., in the consciousness of sin, or "humble," in a general sense, as humility passes in Scripture frequently as a human virtue so very acceptable to God. The gospel writer has chosen as the first epithet the Greek word "praos"—as used (radically) in the Sepuagint of Zechariah IX. 9, for the Hebrew "ani"—instead of "tapeinos," according to the Greek version of Isa. LXVI. 2, where this word is employed to render the same Hebrew term. This would, indeed, in itself not make much difference, as all those concepts are kindred and merge into one another. We could even account for the gospel writer's twofold adoption from the Greek version of words rendering the Hebrew "ani" in this point of view, which is so well borne out by N. T. sources, that this Hebrew term was deep-settled in the minds of Christian believers as being the proper signature of the Messiah. Yet we cannot reconcile in our mind that, if the phrase, as it appears in the gospel, was really used by Jesus, he should have purposed to change the exact phraseology of the Isaianic text which, as aforesaid, he doubtless had in his thought when employing the phrase according to the gospel.

If this objection should appear too nice, we will bring forward another which, we think, cannot consistently be considered so. We mean, that Jesus' self-assertion of the above-cited traits of character conflict, in very substance, with the otherwise so variously and, let us also say, authentically attested "meekness and humility" peculiar to his nature and temper of mind. It is not well conceivable that Jesus should have lauded himself in that manner. He would by it have almost negatived the true essence of his character for those virtues. That the gospel writer should have wished to thus carry out the character of Jesus we can readily understand. For such description would answer to the Christianly predominant view on the Messiah construed from that passage of Zechariah, also from Isa. XLII. 1-3. But in the mouth of Jesus, and applied to himself, the expression, "I am meek and lowly at heart," must sound too strange altogether. If the synoptist had recounted the affirmation by Jesus: "for I am he of whom it is said, "I am meek and lowly at heart" (alluding to Isa. LXV. 2 and Zech. IX. 9 combined), viz., the Messiah, we could promptly assent to the representation imputed to him in the gospel. For, as already indicated, such idea was integrantly woven up in the Messianic texture held by Jesus and those others who put an utter self-renouncing meaning on that phrase of Zechariah. But against the account as it actually stands in the gospel we have the irrepressible objection, that it jars too decidedly with the ordinary conception of real human meekness and humility.

We may further remark in this place that the sense of *resignation* is not at all implied in that picture of the Messianic king produced by Zechariah. He is there, truly, characterized as lowly, yet none the less also as a mighty sovereign with a world-wide dominion. That this dignity had to be supported by a commensurate superior tone and attitude, and that it required a most active, even aggressive policy and procedure, goes without saying. A passively and piously resigned kingly personage could not possibly have done justice to the tremendous task adjudged to the Messiah according to his real portraiture given by the prophet, that he, namely, had to prove himself a valiant conqueror of the Gentiles and, then, an imperial arbiter.

Again, a modest peace ruler the Messiah will in the sense of the prophet be indeed, yet he will doubtless also guard his supreme mundane sovereignty with the unyielding persistence suitable to it. His high self-consciousness will never foresake him.

Nor can we by any means concur in the more modern critical exegesis which detects in the ani "lowly" of

Presages of a Coming Golden Era of Peace. 97

Zech. IX. 9, a monarch who will come from the "class of the oppressed pious" (so Nowack, in loco, after Wellhausen), or that the figure of the expected Messiah was in that passage raised into that of a "spiritual personage," with the character of a real "king almost disappearing" (Giesebrecht, in Nowack). No; we have positively to repudiate such hypercritical notion, fabricated in conformity with the new-fangled allegation of those scholars, that the passage is to be fixed at a much later date than the lifetime of the real prophet, I. Zechariah.

We are wearied by the headlong exegesis of those modern 'higher critics.' They, many of them, are at any time ready to construct a line of novel premises and then deduce from them any notion, set against authentic statements, or local or analogous evidences to the contrary. The most accredited matter of fact of Scripture, believed as such for centuries, and that not only of unthinking credulity, but of subsequent rational judgment as well, they treat often as a mere fabric of ancient ignorance or deficient knowledge, if not of wilful, though disguised, deception. The motive for all this can be no other than a scientific whim which goads them on to their dazzling innovations. When their deductions are accomplished, then the process of Scriptural reconstruction begins—to end nowhere, or in chaos. It is curious to observe how they deal with refractory opposites which confront them, and often very obdurately, to make them fit into their logical schemes. But to our subject. We remark that among the 'higher critics' of more recent times the eminent writer, Stade, stands out in the instance in point as its most correct exponent, proving for this once at least a conservative leaning. In the 'Zeitschrift für die alttest. Wiss.' (1881), he discovers rightly in Zechariah IX. 9, the picture of a victorious Messianic conqueror of the Gentiles, who at the same time choses to dispense with all external magnificence before his own people. This ideal king is a pacific ruler, which he can well be, after having brought under all the pagan principalities.

Of the older critical expositors, Hitzig's rather identical view deserves notice. He finds the same ideal king understood in that passage of Zechariah whom Micah celebrates (ch. V). Jehovah, he interprets, has succored this Messiah in the sweeping warfare against those heathens, carried on by him as the national captain under the heavenly leader. This he finds expressed in the two conjoined predicates tsaddik wenosha "just and having salvation." The immediately following representation is to him also closely combined in sense. This is, that the Messiah proves himself an "ani," viz., he manifests a gentle and pacific disposition. Of this he gives public evidence by riding on the patient and modest animal of peace, and not on the proud, martial horse.

This is indeed the only tenable apprehension of the passage in question. As resting upon this only sound foundation of logical thought and provable analogy, the critics ought for ever to leave it alone. And why should a servilely self-abnegating spirit, or a lowly, passively enduring personal and social attitude be forced upon that ideal king of Zechariah? Because this prophet choses to deviate from the idea other prophets had of the dignity becoming the sublime monarch of the future? (Compare Jer. XVII. 25; XXII. 4; Isa. IX. 5.) If Zechariah, as it may well be supposed, could not find in his heart to swing the ideal king into the awful height into which the exuberant fancy of Isaiah exalted him, even to the degree of apotheosis; if our prophet recognized it as a higher merit that the Messiah should move on a footing with the multitude of his subjects and pass on the lowly level of a rider on donkey back, is it not at once reasonable and fair to allow him the privilege of having formed such distinct idea of his own? This idea would even prove much more attractive to us than that assumed by other prophets. A mighty monarch who disdains stateliness and splendor and prefers discreet simplicity, enlists our sympathy so much more readily and sincerely. A ruler who holds it enough to represent the divine rule of right rather than affect the divine right of rule, wins the admiration of his people and of the world. However this may be, Zechariah was assuredly as much entitled to his notion on the Messiah, as other prophets were to theirs. His depiction varied, indeed, from theirs in the respects we mentioned. Yet, on the other hand, what Zechariah would not deviate from was, we contend, the indigenous, historically inalienable Hebrew idea that the Messiah was to be a powerful monarch from the family of David, with a proud dominion—for all his disdain of domestic splendor—expanded "unto the ends of the earth." On this compare our previous note 18.

(24). That the second advent was the paramount end of his Messianic endeavor, and that he laid on it the greatest stress, must never be doubted. This point can be supported by the most convincing N. T. evidences. It is true that his present activity was by him represented as already forming part of the impending stupendous manifestation of his Messianic government, at his coming again. It was in this sense, too, that he announced the kingdom as already come (see Matt. XII. 28; Luke XVII. 21), though he was then actually but preparing it. Yet it is open to no question that the principal proof and the very pith of Messianic power and glory consisted in his mind in the event of his Messianic return, which he was all along sternly avowing as from an all-engrossing motive of his soul.

(25). See on this important point Keim (l. c. II. 291 sq. and IV. 50 sq.). He proposes, on the whole, that at an earlier phase Jesus announced the kingdom yet as future, while later, when success had strengthened his position, he proclaimed a present kingdom (as he declares apparent from Matt. IV. 17 and XII. 28); also, that Jesus "kept the kingdom suspended between the future and the present." This view may commend itself best to the earnest inquirer who seeks to form an adequate judgment on the point in question.

(26). There is no concealing the fact that there is in this calling away of disciples from their families, which meant in the mind and words of Jesus unquestionably a total and unconditional self-surrender to him, a marked extremity which we with our modern habits of mind can scarcely estimate aright. It is best accounted for by the glow of his Messianic consciousness and the unflinching determination with which he pursued his Messianic end. To these mental and emotional conditions is, we think, also attributable Jesus' demand, repeatedly put to his would-be followers, to dispossess themselves of all material goods, that they might acquire a claim to the

Presages of a Coming Golden Era of Peace. 101

kingdom (or to "salvation ;" see Matt. XIX. 25). The motive for such demand was either that they would secure such claim by the merit of the voluntary dispossession itself (as it is very difficult for a rich man to enter the kingdom of heaven: Matt. XIX. 23), or by the supererogation of selling what they had and giving the proceeds to the poor. The latter motive seems to have been predominant, possibly exclusive, in Jesus' thought, whenever he urged others to sell their earthly belongings and follow him, even where he did not expressly mention the disposal of the price to the poor, as we find it, for instance, in Matt. XIII. 44. Here the advice to "give to the poor" may have to be supplied from ch. XIX. 21. On this point, most interesting though it is, we cannot dwell. What we wish to mark here particularly is, that the renunciation of material possessions asked by Jesus was presumably due to the same ardent Messianic self-feeling which made him obtain followers at the cost of severing family ties.

Renan, 'Life of Jesus,' speaks of this as "throwing down defiance to nature." In whatever light we may view it, we have to admit that it involved a grave question. For, as already above noted, the abandonment of families commanded the disciples by Jesus was absolute and unqualified (see especially Luke IX. 59-62). It was, too, confessedly accomplished by all the twelve apostles (see Matt. XIX. 27). Jesus had held out to them for such sacrifice the transcendent compensation that they would be his coadjutors at the Last Judgment which he would conduct at the coming 'renewal' of things. Likewise he promised exceeding reward, here and hereafter, to every follower who would for his name's sake part from his nearest of kin (ibid. 28, 29).

The position Jesus maintained on this problem was, that the disciple must own no other relationship but to him, and that affection, undivided and undiverted, was due to him alone. For further illustrations marking out Jesus' temper and disposition in the manner of acquiring disciples we refer to Luke XIV. 26, and Matt. XVI. 24, 25. To this range of sentiments belong also the "strong words"—the phrase is Alford's—of Matt. VIII. 22 (compare Luke IX. 59, 60), and likewise Matt. XII. 46-50.

(27.) Fürst (l. c.) says in regard to the "great threatening oracle" running through chapters II-IV of Isaiah: "Framing his lofty oracle with these foreign (i. e. borrowed) fragments (viz., ch. II. 2-4 and IV. 2-6) as prologue and epilogue, Isaiah wished to keep awake the beautiful theocratic hopes and prospects, to console (the people) beforehand on the imminent judgment he had to preach." The same view is substantially held by Gesenius (Commentary on Isaiah, p. 173 ff.) who contends, moreover, for the whole intervening oracle being of one cast. Reuss too ('History of the Sacred Writings of the O. T.') coincides in that view. He summarily denotes the prologue (ch. II. 2-4) as the "prospect of a peaceful federation of the nations on Mt. Zion," and says that "this perspective recurs again, in a somewhat different form, at the end (ch. IV. 2 ff.). The "utterances between those bright initial and final passages," he observes, "were depictions of the moral depravity of the present which deferred the coming of the better times."

Now as to verses 2-4 of ch. II., which most if not

Presages of a Coming Golden Era of Peace. 103

all expositors regard as the heading of the following oration—and we ourselves, too, understood it so in the present treatise—we are tempted to suggest the possibility that they were, at least originally, not intended as such exordium, but as the ending of ch. I. In the latter part of this chapter, vv. 21-31, a terrible chastisement is denounced—though it purports to be a partial one only. It is in fierceness comparable to that threatened by Micah III. 12, which had notoriously (see Jer. XXVI. 18) struck such profound dismay into the hearts of the hearers. (See on this Stade, l c.) It is accordingly quite conceivable that the prophet or his editor chose those mitigating words of promise to set them off against the previous discourse of threatening.

Let us say here that such proceeding would, on the whole, have been quite in keeping with the general prophetic wont. This was, to attach words of consolation to the threatenings they were impelled to pronounce. Even Gesenius, who, as above noted, holds that the passage in point is a prologue, remarks otherwise, that "the Messianic representations always terminate, never commence, the oracles; and, withal, they stand rarely alone." It is indeed provable from many portions of the prophetic writings that it was with them a sort of canon to close their severe monitions and threatenings with some consolatory words. We will quote one parallel, and a very significant one, in several respects. It is Amos, ch. IX. 8, 15. The prophet threatens Israel's deportation by enemies and the destruction of the wicked of them in the exile, but holds out also a happy restoration under a Davidic king, in whose reign prosperity and plenty will prevail. Certainly, the supposition must here be supplied from a parallel occurring in Micah V. 6, 7, that the exiled wicked would in the enemy's country fall by the sword, so that the restoration would be the lot of the deserving remnant only. Yet this does not immediately bear on the point we wish here to mark. We aim to produce one out of many evidences illustrative of what may safely be called a settled motive of the prophets' sentiment, to conciliate on the spot the jarred feelings of the hearers to whom they had to address themselves with gloomy messages of impending divine retribution. But, we maintain, it was with them not a matter of sentiment only. It was part of their mode of reflection and line of thought generally. Hitzig remarks most properly (in his commentary on Malachi), that "the prophetic principle was, that immediately upon the catastrophic judgment they pronounced, there would ensue the Messianic government."

In view of all these points of consideration it would appear not at all strange if the verses of Isa. II. 2-4 had originally been intended as the close of ch. I. By such construction we would, too, be able to relieve essentially the sharp contrast of those verses with the context, which we bring forward at a later point of our text and pursue there with that logical precision which a close inquiry into those prophecies necessitates.

As the prophet had in his oration of ch. I. 21-31, clearly and distinctly predicted the divine chastisement as inexorably decreed only upon the irreclaimable wicked, principally the unscrupulous and corrupt rulers (ibid 24, 28); as he had expressly indicated in v. 25 (as in ch. IV. 4) a sifting judgment, that is, one to be visited on the supposably incorrigible class only, while he held out expressly to the righteous and the penitent middlings that they would be spared and saved (v. 27): it would seemingly suit so much better to take the words of promise which are now found in ch. II. 2-4, as a consolatory appendage to the preceding chapter.

The feelings of the hearers, who almost all of them belonged doubtless to both the last-named classes, could not have been seriously jarred by the denunciation of a judgment which would not be visited on them personally, as the prophet had declared them, some directly, and others conditionally, exempt from it. They could consequently construe the words of promise used by the prophet immediately afterwards, as affixed for their own benefit, and even take them in the sense of restriction to their own enjoyment (or that of their equally deserving posterity). They might have judged so, however general a stamp of national prosperity that bright passage of promise bears in an independent point of view and from its unqualified language and tone. We hazard the entire foregoing hypothesis and submit it for the judicious pondering of those interested in the subject.

(28.) Gesenius, whom we may confidently follow as one of the most scientific and at the same time unbiased commentators of Isaiah, puts chapter I. at the time of the ruinous invasion of Judah by the armies of the allied kings of Israel and Syria, 738-734 B. C. (Commentary, p. 147). Chapters II. and III. he dates almost with it, assuming only a "somewhat anterior time" for them (ibid. p. 176). He proposes that their contents fit alike into the reign of Uzziah and Jotham, and also into the earlier years of Ahaz' reign. To the latter point of time he fixes that Syro-Israelitish war (p. 268). Even chapter V. he sets down as synchronizing with the previous ones. The incisive threat of chastisement through foreign powers set forth in it he fitly construes as alluding to Assyria. This great-power passed as the penal instrument appointed by Jehovah to visit it upon the Judeans for their irreligion and depravity. He does it upon the analogy of ch. VII. 20-25 and VIII. 6-8, where the Assyrian is expressly mentioned. This great-power was to him supposably implied in the prophet's foreboding of ch. V. 26-30.

Let us say that it becomes all the more likely that the prophet had in ch. V. thought of Assyria as the power which was to inflict the penal visitation upon Judah, as we learn, further, from the vehement expostulation he had with king Ahaz (ch. VII. 17, 20-25), that that foreign power was in those days uppermost in his mind. In the last place, as in ch. VIII. 6-8, it is expressly designated. The threatened warlike invasion pictured in ch. V. did indeed not come about. Assur came not as Judah's foe to reduce and ruin him. He came as a friend to offer him relief. Yet the non-fulfillment of that threatening does not signify aught against the decided prevalence in Isaiah's mind of the grave possibility of its realization, and this because of his clear and wise insight into the political constellation of that time.

29. See also Sayce, 'The Times of Isa.,' p. 42, where he observes: "Isaiah was not very old before Judah had reason to know that a new and terrible

power had arisen on the banks of the Tigris." He refers to the presumed alliance of the Judean king Uzziah with Hamath, in 742, which he accepts as a certain event; compare our note 30. Cheyne, 'Introduction to the Book of Isaiah,' says (on ch. VII.): "Isaiah came forward as a young prophet (according to ch. VI. 1) in the year of the death of Azariah, that warlike and enterprising monarch, who ventured to defy Assyria by heading a confederacy of discontented Syrian powers."

(30). Sayce, 'Life and Times of Isaiah,' treats of the alliance between Uzziah and Hamath against Assyria, in the reign of Tiglath-Pileser III., in B. C. 742, as an indubitable fact (p. 42). So do some other Assyriologists. They find their main support for this historical assumption in an extant cuneiform inscription which has been discovered intact on a tablet of Tiglath-Pileser himself. From it they decipher the name of the Judean king Azariah-Uzziah. However, Winckler ('History of Israel in single Essays,' 1895) disputes the identity of that name in the document, and declares the conclusion drawn from it erroneous.

Into the question of the authenticity or probability of the entire hypothesis of Uzziah's coalition with Hamath against Assyria, we cannot enter, nor do we feel ourselves competent enough to deal with it. Suffice it to observe in this place that there is no Biblical reference for it, nor any chance of making it plausible from any portion of Hebrew Scripture, as little as any Scriptural support can be brought for the other cuneiform account of Hezekiah's coalition with Ashdod against Assyria in the reign of Sargon, in B. C. 711.

To verify these suppositions from external sources which have to speak for themselves, comes within the province of Assyriologists only. We must modestly forbear to decide or even suggest whether they can stand their ground in the face of utter Scriptural silence. It may yet be noted that Sayce gives it further on (p. 72), that the Judean king, Uzziah, had to buy Tiglath-Pileser off "by the offer of submission and the payment of tribute." That the issue was really such is not concurred in by some other Assyriologists. We judge of this by the remark of Hildebrandt, in his excellent monograph, 'Judah's Relation to Assyria in Isaiah's Time,' p. 10. He says there—upon the authority of the earlier Assyriologists—that "king Azariah himself was not subjected to the great-king."

(31). The dread of the Assyrian, it is important to notice, was in the air, and had been so already before Tiglath-Pileser's campaign of B. C. 734.

See Kuenen on Amos, whose prophetic activity he puts at B. C. 760-750, the last half of Jeroboam II.'s reign. He explains that the prophet's prediction of a fearful judgment impending on Isreal, alluded to the warlike Assyrian "approach" to Palestine already then attempted. In this view Robertson Smith ('The Proph. of Isr., p. 130) also coincides. He says: "It is plain that Amos has Assyria in his mind, though he never mentions the name. It is no unknown danger that he foresees; Assyria was fully within the range of his political horizon."

(32). We are not alone in setting out emphatically the harsh contrast of Isa. II. 2-4, and the kindred prophetic passages, with their respective contexts.

Presages of a Coming Golden Era of Peace. 109

Kuenen (l. c. p. 36-38) urges it also, though only in a general way. "All attempts," he says, "to construe a coherence between the bright picture of the future given in those verses of Isaiah and the subsequent denunciations have failed." It is for this reason that he assumes their later insertion by a *compiler* who, as he further suggests, gave them the eminent place they occupy in the transmitted text, in the supposition that they came from Isaiah, and attributed to them, as he well might, such great importance.

It is this scrutiny of Kuenen's that dealt likewise with a similar passage of promise in the same prophet. It is the noted and often discussed prospect of restoration immediately subsequent upon the dismal threatening of Isa. ch. XXXII. In this place the ruin of the land is pronounced, and close upon it, in v. 15, the quickening hope of restoration, by miraculous intervention, is held out. This is to Kuenen too incongruous to be tolerated, if an Isaianic origin of the passage were to be maintained. To meet this difficulty he fixes upon its different authorship, and declares it as spurious (ibid. p. 81).

Robertson Smith (l. c.) passes lightly over this "mingling" of opposite pictures of stern rebuke and bright promise of "peace and felicity." Commenting upon Isa. XXIX.-XXXII., which chapters bear upon the imminent crisis of Sennacherib's invasion of Judea, he advances this sentiment: "And so he (Isaiah) draws once more the old contrast between the immediate prospect of a land desolated by invading hosts. . . . . and the days of Israel's restoration" (the latter he does in ch. XXXII. 15). This is, we own, a very pleasant reflection. But we have at the same time to declare it in no way adequate to help clearing off the difficulty before us. It is too uncritically sentimental. We can not hold the old contrast any more reasonably justifiable than the new.

In an interesting, even charming way, George Adam Smith ('The Book of Isaiah') dilates on the opposites in question. He ascribes the lines of ch. II. 1-5 to Isaiah, the Idealist, and ch. II. 6—IV. 1, to Isaiah, the Realist. He says, under the former head, that it is peculiar to "all men who have shown our race how great things are possible," that they "have had their inspiration in dreaming of the impossible. . . . Isaiah was no exception to this human fashion. His first vision was that of a Utopia. . . . He lifts up to us a very grand picture of a vast commonwealth created in Jerusalem. . . . The prophet's own Jerusalem shall be the light of the world, the school and temple of the world; the seat of the judgment of the Lord, when he shall reign over the nations, and all mankind shall dwell in peace beneath Him. It is a glorious destiny. . . It seems to the young prophet's hopeful heart as if at once that ideal would be realized, as if by his own word he could lift his people to its fulfillment. But that is impossible, and Isaiah perceives so as soon as he turns from the far-off horizon to the city at his feet, as soon as he leaves to-morrow alone and deals with to-day. The next verses of the chapter— from v. 6 onwards—stand in strong contrast to those which have described Israel's ideal." He sets forth these contrasts at some length, and then brings out Isaiah under the other head, "The Realist," in reference to ch. II. 6-IV. 1.

Now while we have to accord these agreeable lines the merit of unusual suggestiveness, it is, on the other hand, plain that they do not help us in any way over the grave difficulty of the opposites of sense afforded in the orations of Isaiah under discussion. It is impossible for us to improve his distinction between ideal and real, as we have to deal with the positive contrast confronting us there. We cannot possibly and sensibly say, that Isaiah's mood and tendency of mind were to-day, when he gave forth the piercing denunciations, overcome by the impression of present sad realities, and to-morrow again elated to the eminences of ideal vision. It is utterly inconceivable that one is at a certain period of his life both an idealist and realist within a few days apart from one another. This is not borne out by the experience of men.

We know of no reasonable means by which those contrary utterances could be reconciled, so long as they continue in their delivered sequence to be credited to the prophets under whose literary names they appear. Even the expedient of finding a mitigation of such contrast in the theory that the promise of a brilliant national future applies only to a saved remnant after the threatened doom will have been executed, does in our view not hold, at least not in regard to expressions such as are used in Isa. II. 2-4, and the like prophetic oracles (see on this, our text). In that passage of Isaiah a gorgeous outlook for the future is wedged in between penal denunciations and the threat of a judgment to be visited on the Judeans. That the prophet meant every word he spoke, is not to be doubted. The language he used is too marked to be mistaken. The best commentators are agreed upon this. There is a settled consensus among them that Isaiah had firmly rooted in his mind the necessary infliction of a penal calamity on his compatriots by the mighty Assyrian ever since the reign of Ahaz, and down to the time of Sennacherib's invasion.

It is in particular Stade ('History, etc.') who asserts in the most positive manner that Isaiah's and Micah's conviction until then was, that the fatal day of visitation would irrevocably befall the land and its capital. Similarly Sayce and Robertson Smith assume. The latter says, that "Isaiah alone (of all the other non-prophetic Judean people) was during these thirty years (which elapsed since his notable interview with king Ahaz) assured that no combination could stem the tide of (Assyrian) conquest." And it is in view of this indisputable circumstance of the prophet's sure foreboding of that eventuality, which clashes, however, so very sharply with his alleged coextensive promise of a golden era coming, that we dwell in our treatise so decidedly upon the proposition that that bright passage, like the similar ones of other Hebrew poetic preachers, is well-nigh rendered of no effect, nay meaningless, either in an historical, exegetical, or dogmatic respect.

The same objection holds of the contrast in Micah IV. 1-4, a contrast against which Stade objects, as already noted elsewhere, that it is "utterly improbable that the prophet should have weakened the impression of his oracle of ch. III. 12 by another of just the contrary import. Kuenen (l. c.) attempts to meet Stade's objection by distinguishing between the written and the spoken word of Micah. He frankly owns that if the oration were to be set down as a spoken one it would certainly have to be declared self-contradictory. Yet he claims that the prophet only committed it to writing, and this makes the difference as to the weight of that contrast. He reasons thus : "It is impossible that Micah should have stopped short at the threatened fall of Jerusalem, viz., in ch. III. 12. He necessarily must also have given voice to the expectations he cherished for the future." We cannot but wonder at such feeble argument produced by that eminent critic, as well as at his most arbitrary distinction between those oracles of the prophet. Where has he found it certified, or how can he even make it probable?

Before we close this argument we remark, that the Messianic hopers of all ages were apparently never troubled by the contrast of those prophetic utterances. The strict and unquestioning adherence to the notion that the Messiah was yet to come at some future time according to a pretended plan of Providence for Israel, shuts out any critical inquiry into relative texts. So it was in old time and in the Middle Ages, and so it is yet among the oppressed Jews of the world generally. Those clinging to the Messianic hope would never dare to approach analytically the essence of this problem, nor be put out by the uncertain or questionable passages of Scripture, which have been traditionally fixed as designating that hazy creation of old Israelitish fancy.

As illustrative of this position, we will quote a few observations from the commentary of Ibn Ezra on Isaiah. This great Toledan of the twelfth century C. E., who is mostly famous as grammarian and Scripture commentator, treats the noted passage of Isa. II. 2-4, in this wise. He lays down as premiss the assurance that in the "after days" of v. 2, reference can be but to the future "days of Messiah" proper. That the prophet could have held in mind no other, previous period as the subject of his forecast, appears, he reasons, from the "fact that there never was a time after Isaiah in which the Israelites were not subject to the ill fate of warfare, carried on against them. For it is variously recorded that even all along the Second Polity of Israel, such warfare had not ceased."

And here he brings forward in a sort of satiric humor: "Even our text itself bears witness to this circumstance, for it says (v. 4), "and they (viz., the Gentile nations) will not learn war any more." What this piquant and enigmatic commentator wished to convey here is not difficult to make out. He undoubtedly aimed to impute to that expression—though scarcely in exegetical earnest—the sense that "they (the Gentiles) will (or do) not need to learn war any more," just because they were keeping themselves in continual practice of it (in their hostility against Israel). That such construction is not really in the spirit of the prophet's phraseology, and that it cannot in the least be taken to bear such meaning, is patent enough, and was unquestionably as clear to Ibn Ezra as it is to us. Yet he found it suitable and gratifying to his gloomy Israelitish mood, and thought it congenial to other Scriptural inquirers for whom he wrote his commentary, to tinge his exposition with a pathetic allusion to the hapless fate of Israel in the past and as well in his own days.

(33). As most instructive in regard to the question of discriminating divine judgment in the prophetic

Presages of a Coming Golden Era of Peace. 115

literature, we have to name the book of Amos. It affords interest to follow this prophet through ch. v. 27, VI. 14, VIII. 8, where his denunciation appears yet in a general tone, to ch. IX., in which the destruction of the wicked Israelites is pronounced and the rescue of the better ones at the same time judiciously guarded. Yet his conclusion was, that the catastrophe of the fall of the Ephraimite State with an attending woeful captivity was divinely determined and had inevitably to befall the good along with the impious. Even the restorative means of grace, national repentance, seems to have passed in his mind as unavailable at that advanced stage of guiltiness. The implication of ch. VIII. 9, 10, at least appears to be, that God would not allow any more that the catastrophe, penally incurred, should somehow be eventually averted. (See on this Hitzig, in loco; also Robertson Smith, I. c., p. 141.)

For the period of the Exile, Ezekiel, ch. XX., is very illustrative on the point of Divine discriminating procedure. The prophet teaches a very close judicial separation in vv. 34-38. The same idea is bodied forth in the Second Isaiah, ch. LXV; LXVI. 24.

A like line of thought and teaching appears in the still later prophet, Malachi. In him the additional element of a "refining" procedure is brought forth. This judicial test is to be applied to each individual [Levite] (ch. III. 2, 3; compare Zech. XIII. 9), whilst a most crushing, dread judgment awaits the (irreclaimable) wicked.

There is in all those cited prophetic passages matter for further thought, which we can, however, not pursue in these pages.

(34). The notion that Isa. II. 2-4 (and likewise Micah IV. 1-4), were inserted by a later compiler of the chapters from II. onwards, is represented by Kuenen (l. c. p. 36-38). Their composition he ascribes to an older contemporary of Isaiah and Micah.

Cheyne, who, with a number of other more recent 'higher critics,' declares it "imprudent to defend the antiquity of the passage," has concluded to attribute it to an editor of Isaiah, and one who lived after the Exile. The authorship itself he fixes as the "work of a post-Exilic imitator of the older prophets" ('Introd. to the Book of Isa.').

Similarly Stade judges (in Zeitschr., 1881, as above). Yet, while he disallows positively the old date of the Assyrian epoch, he is not so dogmatic about the lateness of its origin. He cannot decide as to this question, but inclines to an indefinite date of its writing and incorporation, holding it possible that it succeeded the lifetime of Ezekiel, but no less possible that it may have to be put earlier.

(35). It is proper to remark that if our proposition, presented in note 27, should hold, the contraries of the gloom of denunciation and glow of promise, closely joined to one another in Isaiah's oration, could be reconciled without much difficulty. This proposition is, that the verses 2-4, were an epilogue to the antecedent chapter. Having discussed it there at some length, we need only briefly refer to it here.

(36). Where righteousness is the guiding principle, there peace must necessarily result or subsist, as the same prophet has so beautifully said in ch. XXX. 17, "and the outcome of righteousness will be peace." The ideal

Presages of a Coming Golden Era of Peace. 117

king will go forth to govern, "girded with righteousness" (ch. XI. 5). Thus he will not need to smite with the sword. His mere word will be the rod of rule, and as well of chastisement of the refractory element. His mere breath will penally strike down the incorrigible evildoer (v. 4). This is, truly, totally different from the ordinary human discipline. It is a sort of supernatural judicature. But then is not the illustrious vicegerent of Jehovah otherwise divinely gifted? Will he not possess the divine-like capacity of not having to judge by appearance or decide upon auricular evidence, but be able to unravel, with penetrating insight into the very core of the accused, the clear and true facts of each criminal charge? (v. 3; compare 1 Sam. XVI. 7). And surely—as we have to infer from the cognate and, as we think it indisputable, also connate passage, ch. IX. 5, 6,—the prophet must have wished to apply this sort of immaterial procedure of the ideal Anointed to his external judicature as well. As his sovereign sway is "unlimited," all the other nations will be amenable to his world-tribunal located in the Judean capital, Jerusalem, where he will execute justice to them in the same spiritual manner in which he judges his own people.

It will be pertinent to add here the remark that the apocalyptic IV. Ezra has given forth the sentiment, that the Messiah will need no arms, but be able to destroy whole armies of enemies arrayed in battle against him, with his fiery breath, and the flames and sparks shooting from his lips and tongue. It admits of no question that the Isaianic expression of ch. XI. 4, underlies that mystical writer's Messianic description. He elaborated it, putting in the effective stroke of the spiritual 'mitrailleuse.' It is, we are yet to observe, a fact which must strike every inquirer into the apocalyptic books of Enoch and IV. Ezra, that both these writers drew substantially from ch. XI. of Isaiah, which served as a model for 'far-off' mystical imagery to other old inquirers as well.

(37). The Second Isaiah has borrowed the image of the pacification of the brutes in the blessed future, in ch. LXV. 25. Yet he left out the second clause of v. 9, "for the earth shall be full of the knowledge of the Lord, as the waters cover the sea." About this omission we bring no complaint. On the contrary, it seems quite proper. For in connection with the brutes, it can easily be seen, the knowledge (and acknowledgment) of God is not readily conceivable. The only acceptable sense of this connection would appear to be that in which Delitzsch (Commentary, in loco,) construes it, viz., that Jehovah will in that happy and glorious Messianic future turn the fierce temper of all the noxious beasts, as their quality of doing injury as a penal visitation upon sinners will then not be needed any more, the presumption being that all the inhabitants of the "land" (of Israel) will "know" him and, consequently, serve him with steadfast purpose. But this is, we object, too forced a meaning. The second clause, taken as an explanation of the first in such indirect bearing, is thus not at all plain. It needs a philosophical interpreter to make its sense clear. The prophet, we hold, cannot reasonably be supposed to have spoken thus enigmatically.

The more natural implication would indeed be, that God would at that future happy time infuse a certain degree of intellect and suitable understanding into the

Presages of a Coming Golden Era of Peace. 119

nature of the animals, so that they would by their own discretion live in peace mutually and towards men. But why, then, express such improvement of the rudimentary animal intelligence under the phrase of "knowing Jehovah?" And yet there seems no alternative but to take the whole picture of animal pacification in this point of view. Jehovah would then be represented as newly capacitating the brutes to comprehend his will, which would be, that they should all be tame and mild and do no more hurt of any kind.

That this sense is not so foreign to an old prophet, is shown by the analogue of the prophet Hosea. He holds out to Israel a period of blissful restoration coming, in which they would live again secure and free from fear. God would eventually not only "break the battle" with its deadly instruments "out of the land," but also "make a covenant" for the behoof of re-accepted Israel "with the beasts of the field, etc.," that is, bind them, as it were, by oath to abstain from every injury to his people (ch. II. 20). In the figurative language of Scripture, this means that Jehovah will not only transform, by his creative and fashioning power, the violent nature of the wild beasts into a milder one, but will even personally interpose his address to them and direct them how they shall henceforth conduct themselves. That Jehovah does not reject such mode of approaching animals for certain ends of his government and providence, can be supported by various Scriptural examples.

Upon the point of the many parallels in external literature of features of the gentle, peaceable, even friendly disposition of animals in idyllic pictures of the golden age past and expected to be again, also those still more fabulous ones of a golden age ever present—at the distant terrestrial Islands of the Blessed—we cannot dwell, however desirable it might be to do so.

(38). For this, by the way, there was a scant prospect. The exile of the masses from the ruined kingdom of Israel was then already accomplished. It was not at all likely that the all-powerful Assyrian would give up the Israelitish captives at the mandate of any Messianic ruler of Jerusalem.

(39). Kuenen (l. c. p. 53) remarks, too, that the prospective sanguine vengeance upon Israel's hostile neighbors "ill harmonizes with Isaiah's uniformly ideal perception of the future."

(40). Cheyne, 'The Prophets of Isr., (1895), brings forward the two possible alternatives of meaning to be put on Isaiah's description of the everlasting permanence of the domination of Messiah: the one, that he would have "an uninterrupted succession," and the other, that he would be "immortal." He inclines to the latter construction, as being "more in accordance with the general tenor of the description." We cannot go along with him in this estimate. It is true, Isaiah has in both places, here and in ch. XI., given to the portraiture of Messiah transcendent enough colors. One expression at least, as to the ideal king's name, is positively too exorbitant a sublimation to be countenanced even in a prophet, viz., "the mighty God" (or "a mighty God"). And it is only in this view, too, that we may partially allow for it, that it is, namely, but metaphorical and applied simply to the name and not the nature of Messiah. Yet against the assumption that the Messiah's immortality, that is, his undying state

Presages of a Coming Golden Era of Peace. 121

on earth, was intended in our passage, there stand out, first, numerous instances in Scripture in which the everlasting endurance of a Hebrew monarch on his terrestrial throne is asserted, all of which can imply only an endless succession in his family. Again, we can, for all Isaiah's extravagant designation of the ideal king's qualities and dignity, never bring ourselves to suppose for one moment that he aimed to represent him as really to be transformed from a human into a supernal being, with the unnaturally distinct prerogative of having an undying nature. Lastly, we hold it inconceivable that Isaiah should, even for once, have set himself against the organic conception and fundamental principle of Hebrew Scripture, which is, that every man, however high or holy, must die: see Gen. III. 19, 22; Ps. LXXXIX. 49. This principle stands too strongly and decidedly in the way of taking Isa. IX. 6, as indicative of immortality, were it even otherwise admissible to give it such a meaning. It alone would be enough to confute Cheyne's so very singular preference of interpretation.

We are yet to remark that the question of later, apocalyptic apprehensions of the Messiah's deathless immortality on earth, cannot enter into the rational consideration of an old prophetic expression like Isa. IX. 6. On this point we cannot enlarge. For details on it we refer to the significant passage of John XII. 32; also Volkmar's 'Introd. to the Apocr.,' II., IV. Ezra, p. 398, and Langen, 'Judaism in Palestine in the Time of Christ,' p. 416.

EXCURSUS.

While on the subject of prophetic enthusiasm and excitement of brightest hope for the national future of Israel at particular auspicious points of time in their history, it occurred to us that as a most suitable instance the passage of Isa. IX. 1-6 may be noted. As great importance has ever been attached to this passage by Messianic inquirers, we deem it proper to reflect upon it at length, that we may draw from it such pertinent illustration as a rational apprehension of its entire text may enable us.

As to the vexed question what personage the prophet may have alluded to, we freely declare that it is to us satisfactorily enough settled. We hold it incontestably certain that the prophet thought of none other than king Hezekiah. The other point, what immediate occasion and time may have inspired those lines, is not so easy of solution. Let us say that an interesting key to it has been furnished in a meritorious monograph written by Hildebrandt, 'Judah's Relations to Assyria in Isaiah's Time,' 1874. Now while we will ultimately disagree with him on the chief part of his hypothesis, viz., that the noted passage was written not long after king Hezekiah's accession, and that the exultant lines of verse 3 had direct reference to his revolt against Assyria, yet his suggestions are so very striking and applicable

Presages of a Coming Golden Era of Peace. 123

in spirit that we may safely reproduce them in the main for the purpose of the desirable illustration. Moreover, we will subsequently adduce the remarks of a distinguished theological scholar which accord with his sentiments on the point we wish to bring out in this place. Hildebrandt has gone critically into the modernly discovered and improved Assyrian sources, by the aid of which he endeavored to set right various doubtful or conflicting accounts of the Biblical record. Hezekiah's revolt * is by him, as by most Assyriologist interpreters

---

*That this was the first actual revolt of Hezekiah may be taken for granted on the strength of this argument of Kuenen's alone ('Introduction to the Books of the O. T.', II. p. 30 ff. and p. 53), that there is in the numerous inscriptions from Sargon's time but one that mentions 'Judah,' and this means nothing else than the Judean king's vassalage to Assyria, but not his reduction by force of arms. Had this been accomplished there would, as that writer most sensibly argues, have certainly been left a trace of it in those numerous Assyrian documents. But this is not the case. Kuenen maintains this position expressly against Cheyne ('Prophecies of Isaiah') who, he says, "assumes wrongly that Hezekiah had been at war with Sargon." Stade too ('History of the People of Israel') holds that Hezekiah was, from the silence of Assyrian inscriptions about Palestinian affairs in the reign of Sargon, acquiescent under this great-king. Among more recent Assyriologists, Winckler ('History of Israel in single Essays' p. 182) contends however for a general Palestinian uprising, and one lasting for three years, from B. C. 713 to 711. It was headed by the Philistian state of Ashdod. He infers—making his own interpretation of respective Assyrian data (p. 224), that all Philistia, Judah, Edom and Moab had joined in the Ashdod revolution. He assigns it as fomented by a domestic Egyptian party. Hezekiah, he advances, "could not resist either the temptation or coercion to take part in the insurrection undertaken in the trust in Egyptian succor." Sayce too, in 'The Times of Isaiah,' assumes a Sargonic-Judean conflict in B. C. 711, despite the

of the respective circumstances,* connected with the time of Sennacherib's accession, B. C. 705. It was after the assassination of his father and predecessor, the great-king Sargon, that many vassal states east, north and south moved sympathetically to revolt from Assyria and throw off the chafing yoke of tributary dependence upon it. The reduction of Merodach-Baladan, of Babylon, had occupied Sennacherib's activity till about B. C. 701, when he decided to march forward to southwestern Asia to re-subject the revolted countries.† He

---

utter silence about it in the Hebrew records. He invents an allusion to it in chapter X. and XI. of Isaiah. The prophecy of these chapters he conjectures as having been called forth by Sargon's supposed movement against Jerusalem. Pursuantly to this hypothesis he has to propose an alteration of the text of 2 Kings XVIII. 13, where "the twenty-fourth year" is to be substituted for "the fourteenth year." We cannot here enter upon a discussion of this entire hypothesis of that great English scholar. Robertson Smith (l. c. p. 296, sq.) brings very valid arguments against it, proving its "extreme improbability."

A sort of middle view is upheld by Rawlinson (as above), who leaves it uncertain "whether Hezekiah was engaged personally in this war." Yet he accredits the relative Assyrian inscription sufficiently to judge therefrom that Hezekiah "appears to have (then) been prepared to cast off the Assyrian yoke." He decides, though, that "it seems most probable that there was no actual conflict between Assyria and Judaea until after the accession of Sennacherib" (p. 187).

*See also Winckler, l. c.

†Whether or how far Egypt had abetted and co-operated in this wide-spread anti-Assyrian uprising is regarded disputable by Winckler, ibid. p. 97. Other writers, among them Rawlinson and Stade, consider it unquestionable that Egypt had actively and eagerly joined in the general movement against Assyria. The latter writer holds firmly that back of all these Palestinian states was Egypt, which had in B. C. 704 got in Tirhakah an energetic ruler.

made war upon Phoenicia, Philistia, and, lastly, Judea. King Hezekiah is presumed to have led this western revolution (so Stade, Winckler and others).

Now Hildebrandt advances the proposition that Hezekiah, who was so surpassingly celebrated by the prophet Isaiah, having awakened great rejoicing among the pious Judeans by his vigorous undoing of the mischief his idolatrous father, Ahaz, had wrought in the country, made also the devout prophet's heart "exult loudly over this great triumph of Jehovah, who had by his grace made an end, even without striking a blow, of the thirty years' servitude (to Assyria), and thirty years' idolatry." He lets the prophet utter, in his rapturous estimate of his august friend's coming government, the famous lines of Isa. IX. 1-6, which held out the glorious, blissful era at hand, of which former poet-preachers had dreamt and which had doubtless become traditionally settled as an invaluable oracle of bright and lofty re-assurance for the future. That blessed far-off event, marked in the prophecy of Isa. II. 2-4, was or was about to be realized now. The bliss of the four Messianic p's, peace, prosperity and proud power, was in the prophet's vision really attained with the reign of the marvellously God-endowed Judean king. To such a high pitch of happy anticipation the prophet's imagination was raised!

But, alas, he became very soon—according to Hildebrandt, who puts Hezekiah's revolt indefinitely between B. C. 705 and 701—sorely disappointed in his fond and brilliant vision. To his poignant regret he had found out that idealistic longing was one thing, but that an all-powerful over-lord's practical, summary dealing with a rebellious vassal was quite another. Instead of glorious independence from Assyria and a firm establishment of Jehovah's theocratic government in Jerusalem, conducted by his vicegerent, the Davidic world-emperor, with the Judean capital as the center of gravity for universal rule and universal direction of affairs, there came a sadly blighted hope. Hezekiah had to submit himself to the Assyrian—a submission which brought back the hard feudatory conditions of Judea, and lasted unaltered during all the rest of his lifetime, even that of his son, Manasseh. "The events in Mesopotamia," remarks Hildebrandt pointedly, "soon taught the prophet that the time of eternal peace for the nations of the earth had not taken its so warmly hoped-for beginning."

The lesson was indeed a dismal one for the prophet, the king and the people alike. For—so we are informed by the relative inscriptions which are substantially upheld by the most competent Assyriologists—Sennacherib proceeded with ruthless purpose against Judah, carried by storm the fortifications of the rural towns, and led captive to Assyria many thousands of their inhabitants. A number at least of those towns were cut off from Hezekiah's domain—the bombastic cuneiform inscriptions give out, all—and given to the Philistian vassals who had remained faithful to their suzerain.* Jerusalem had indeed held out gallantly, and her brave and dauntless defenders had successfully beaten back the enemy's fierce onsets, though they could

---

*So Winckler and Hildebrandt. Stade maintains, however: "Yet it seems that he (Hezekiah) did not yield to the giving over of Judean territory to Philistian cities, nay that he even enlarged his own land at their cost."

Presages of a Coming Golden Era of Peace. 127

not prevent the battering of the north gate of the city, and the breach made in it.* The Judean capital was saved with its king and its people,† but a heavy ransom had to be paid for the deliverance, and submission to the oppressive Assyrian vassalage was the final issue.

The prophet's enthusiastic forecasts of a high and glorious Messianic era approaching, given forth in the cognate passages of Isa. II. 2-4, IX. 1-6 and XI. 1-9,

---

*Stade says that the legends of 2 Kings XVIII., XIX., err in that they assume that Jerusalem was not at all assailed, and the officials of Sennacherib had come to the gates of the city only for delivering his messages. Yet he concedes a partial agreement, in other respects, of both the relative Hebrew and Assyrian accounts. The very conservative theologian, Delitzsch, (in Herzog and Plitt's Cyclopedia, article Sennacherib) says: "What the book of Kings jointly with the book of Isaiah says concerning these occurrences, is without difficulty reconcilable with the cuneiform account." Yet he points out, on the one side, the designed concealment in this account of the fatal issue visited upon the division of Sennacherib's army which had besieged Jerusalem, and also a palpable misrepresentation in regard to Hezekiah's tribute; while on the other side he intimates the possibility of having to place an interrogation point after the number 185,000 of the Biblical narrative (2 Kings XIX. 35; Isa. XXXVII. 36), as well as he suggests that the item in Sennacherib's cuneiform account of his deportation of 200,150 Judeans into captivity "seems to deserve greater attention than has so far been given to it." It lies beyond our present purpose to enter at any length into the interesting question of the various apparent divergences and possible agreements between the Biblical and cuneiform narrations of events and incidents bearing on that most important portion of Israel's history.

†Stade observes that, though Judah was deprived of a large part of population, the bulk of her martial men were doubtless concentrated in Jerusalem and were thus saved.

were soon enough confounded and frustrated by the most gloomy and disastrous realities. The turbulence and convulsions Judea sustained by Sennacherib's invasion were, despite the rescue of Jerusalem, a dreadful offset against the earlier vision of the dawn of a bright and golden era of peace being at hand. To see the formerly so highly exalted, beloved king lowered again from the high pedestal of glorious world-rule upon which Isaiah had set him in his transport of personal admiration for him and high hope for the nation, must have given this lofty seer a most humiliating sensation. Like a dissolving view that happy vision of the past had now vanished, with abashing delusion left behind. The labor of love spent on the dual Messianic message of chpts. IX. 1-6 and XI. 1-9, proved to be wasted already after a short interval, with the re-subjection of the crestfallen Judean king, its central figure and glorified hero. And, however exemplary Hezekiah's government may have been in regard to the furtherance of pure religion and Hebrew literature, however great his merits in every patriotic respect, yet the fancied Messianic glory which Isaiah had prefigured for his reign remained utterly unfulfilled.

Let us here yet quote a kindred remark, and one, as aforesaid, made by a recognized scientific authority. It is Stade, the learned writer of the 'History of the People of Israel,' who, narrowing his similar observations to Isa. II. 2-4, expresses the following sentiments: "The prophet, having strongly and deeply cherished the fundamental expectation that in the "after-days," in which the danger from Assyria would be taken away,

Presages of a Coming Golden Era of Peace. 129

the Messianic empire would be ushered in,* understood practically the failure of the Assyrian attempts upon Jerusalem as such removal of danger. Yet in this he deceived himself. And the more time went on from that decisive year, 701 B. C., the more clearly it was shown that the Messianic empire had not come. In the Judean State the old conditions continued. Nay the disaster which befell the Assyrians in that year, signified all but their destruction through Jahve's power, which Isaiah had predicted. . . . It is true, Jerusalem was not conquered, yet it became dependent again upon the Assyrian great-king, who continued to dominate in Nineveh as the lord of the world." "The king Hezekiah," says Stade in another part of his history, was indeed "not totally vanquished, he was only reduced. Yet he had to own homage and pay tribute again to the Assyrian over-lord as before." Things had fallen out so differently from the glowing imaginations of the prophets!

In particular had Isaiah's oracular trilogy—if we

---

*About the same sentiment Robertson Smith (l. c. p. 300 sq.) expresses in regard to the Messianic picture of Isa. XI. 1-9. Suggesting as date for its composition about B. C. 720, when the Assyrian had accomplished the fall of Samaria and the destruction of the Syrian principalities, and when his further movement would be to execute judgment as Jehovah's instrument upon Judah as well, he lets the prophet foreshow, as ensuing upon that divine judgment, days of blessing under "a new sapling that springs from the old stock of Jesse" (Isa. XI. 1). The "blessings of this Messianic time" would be enjoyed, as coextensive with the fall of the Assyrian, by the "remnant of Israel," (ibid. X. 20) which, thus delivered, would henceforth be awarded the benefits of a "reign of peace and order," as painted in Isa. XI. 1-9.

may call so the at least spiritually interconnected passages of ch. II. 2-4, IX. 1-6 and XI. 1-9—signally failed of accomplishment. The bright hope of seeing the Messianic empire inaugurated with Hezekiah, the monarch after the prophet's heart, who was from the start of his principate so full of promise for a *Davidic* restoration, was now woefully betrayed. Doubtless, it had at the time found a living echo also in the hearts of the rural Judeans. Yet presently they were crushed beneath the weight of (partial) Assyrian conquest. And the Jerusalemites—well, they had gained nothing but the transient feeling of relief from the perils of the siege. At best there was mixed with it a proud consciousness of military valor which proved itself so successful in the unflinching defence of the citizens' homes. But for all that they had no real victory before them. Reduced again as they were to feudal relations with the Assyrian suzerain, they must have felt their success to be but a phantom achievement. Practically, it was a worse defeat than "Sennacherib's signal overthrow*" (so Sayce,

---

*That the direct aim of Sennacherib's campaign of B. C. 701 was Anterior Asia, is the generally accepted notion of those modern scholars who follow the relative cuneiform documents. Reuss ('The History of the Holy Writ of the O. T.') holds, that "the huge armies which Sargon and Sennacherib led into the field, were not directed against impotent Judah," but against Egypt. This is also the positive view of Keil (Commentary, on 1 Kings XVIII. 13), and is in accordance with Herodotus whom he cites there. Keil endeavors to support Herodotus' representation by 2 Kings XIX. 24 and Isa. X. 24. The latter passage seems indeed rather conclusive in favor of this position. He also finds further evidence for it in Tirhaka's military movement to meet Sennacherib's army in battle, recounted in 2 Kings XIX. 9.

Yet, again, there is in our day a difference of view on this

Presages of a Coming Golden Era of Peace. 131

l. c.). For he could soon recover again; but for the hapless Judeans there had been newly forged the chafing chains of hard foreign dependence. If they should before have been carried along by the prophet's eloquent, poetic promises, their spirits were again subdued and cowed, as though those bright oracles had never been spoken. Their charm was broken. The Judeans were now again in as bad a way and as far off from the ideal, Messianic goal as they were before. The oracles, considering the then actual situation, were valueless: for,

---

very movement. Winckler (l. c.) disconnects him entirely with the war of B. C. 701. He assumes another, later expedition of Sennacherib against Palestine and Egypt, which he puts at B. C. 689-81. He contends that the Tirhaka of Scripture belongs to the time of this later Assyrian expedition, and that its fatal issue—which he of course accounts for as the natural affliction of pestilence befalling the army—is chronologically to be interpreted accordingly.

This assumption would, we remark, be in good stead to the smaller number of critics who reject the narratives alike of Herodotus, II. 141, and Isaiah XXXVII. 36 and 2 Kings XIX. 35, even if stripped of the miraculous features, as irreconcilable with the cuneiform accounts, and therefore as mythical. They rest their position upon these Assyrian inscriptions as to the decisive battle of Altaku (Eltekeh) and the subsequent military actions of Sennacherib. According to Winckler's new view, the latter's first expedition could be taken as truly victorious and unmarred by any fatality. The sudden departure of Sennacherib from the besieged city of Jerusalem, again, could be set down as having been caused by the breaking our of new disturbances in Babylonia (which Winkler really suggests). At the same time the Biblical story of the Assyrian fatality could, in the main, be saved—an endeavor which even some Assyriologists have not disdained to make. In conclusion we refer the student to Winer's discussion, in Bibl. Realwörterbuch, s. v. Hezekiah. He offers there a rather plausible solution of the questions involved in the whole subject.

having once failed, they must have failed forever. This is an indisputable truism. And we should, too, keep it always before our eyes in judging of the true merits of those and similar prophetic utterances.

Even if we should distinguish with Robertson Smith (l. c.) between "poetic and ideal constructions," (such as he pronounces Isaiah's "concrete pictures of the future, in which he embodied his faith and hope, to have been from the necessity of the case") and "literal forecasts of the future," which those pictures were not (as he presumes), we would obtain no better results of adjustment of the question. We would not thereby get beyond the sober fact that Isaiah's predictions of the Messianic empire to start up with the princely "child" (ch. IX. 6) of the renowned house of David, had at and through Sennacherib's invasion been brought to naught. The evasive construction put upon them that they were nevertheless Providentially designed to be realized 'in good time,' does not bear the touch of clear, investigating thought. If Providence refused their accomplishment all through the good time of the good king Hezekiah, he cannot consistently be supposed to be more favorably inclined to any other time for the consummation of that national hope of Israel.

At this point we are recalled to Hildebrandt's commentation of Isa. IX. 1-6. We followed his argument to a considerable degree, and along the line of his apprehension of those verses. But we did so as to the sentiments he devolves from them rather than the historic-exegetical construction he assumes for their subject-matter. For we differ essentially from him both as regards the principal motive of this his construction, the chronological one, and the manner of interpreting the relative text. His assumption is—and in this he was guided by the position of some earlier eminent Assyriologists—that Hezekiah's reign began B. C. 706-5, about contemporaneously with Sennacherib's accession, which is authoritatively fixed at 705. Pursuantly he conjectures that Hezekiah's revolt against Assyria fell at a point of time "when he had not long been on the throne," that is, within 705-1. As evidence for the latter hypothesis he adduces 2 Kings XVIII. 7, to which he adapts, as supposably yielding the same chronological sense, Isa. IX. 3-6. Now, we have to object, not only are these passages by themselves not in the least "decisive" conformably to his hypothesis, there stands out against it the more weighty point, that a much earlier date of Hezekiah's accession is warranted by the consensus of the best modern Assyriologists and theological scholars*

---

*The beginning of Hezekiah's reign is variously dated all the way from 728 to ca. 705 B. C. The most competent modern scholars determine upon a chronology yielding a long enough space of time for a well settled state of prosperity in the Jewish land under that noted monarch. More or less of a quarter-century of happy development and splendid prospect for the future may thus be gained. All this seems perfectly consonant, too, with the principal facts of Hezekiah's reign which Hebrew tradition has preserved, and which are only intelligible if a solid and settled peaceable progress is to be presumed as having marked out the earlier part of his reign. A brief space of four years at the most, which would result according to Hildebrandt and those few others who incline to synchronize Sennacherib's and Hezekiah's accessions, could not consistently suffice to create that bright, almost dazzling sign of the times reflected from the pages of sacred history which treat of the events of Hezekiah's reign. The assumption, then, of a fairly long interval

Ingeniously enough, it is true, does he expound the passage of Isa. IX. 1-6*. Yet contrary chronological assurance, and lack of demonstrative evidence as to the textual indication of 2 Kings XVIII. 7, invalidate his sagacious exegetical attempt.

Now when we gain, as we do according to that array of more recent authority, an interval between Hezekiah's accession and his later revolt, which ranges all along from B. C. 728 to 705 or thereabouts, we can easily

---

between its beginning and the revolt against Assyria with its following crisis, is well justified, and we unqualifiedly adhere to it. As a typical Davidic-Messianic age that quarter-century might accordingly have well passed in the exalted vision of the prophet Isaiah who, as we hold, has drawn in those famous passages of chpts. II., IX. and XI., brilliant pictures of happiness and glory which, while they ostensibly foreshadow an ideal prospect into futurity, were effectually shadowing forth the happy aspect of the present.

Now it is Delitzsch who fixes the date of Hezekiah's accession on B. C. 728. Reuss assumes 727. While this date is suggested by 2 Kings XVIII. 10, yet Stade contends, contrarily to this inference, that ibid. ver. 13 must be upheld as paramount. He decides, therefore, on B. C. 715-714 as the date to be authentically set down for the commencement of Hezekiah's reign. Wellhausen and Kuenen concur in this chronology. Cheyne inclines to B. C. 724, and Sayce about the same. The latter's peculiar conjectural position, that the text of 2 Kings XVIII. 13, is faulty and must be amended into the indication of the twenty-fourth instead of the fourteenth year, we have elsewhere brought forward. Winckler marks B. C. 720 as the suitable date.

*Hildebrandt interprets Isa. IX. 5, as an exultation not over the real nativity (of Hezekiah), but his 'royal' birth, in the sense of formal induction into kingship. The phraseology, "For a child is born unto us," he takes, referring to Ps. II. 7, as being a trope signifying God's solemn installation of the prince as Judean king upon his holy mountain.

adjudge likewise about the same extent of time in which Isaiah's composition of ch. IX. 1-6 can have fallen. Accordingly, we advance the following two suppositions for the approximate date of this passage.

TWO SUPPOSITIONS.

Isaiah may have written it at Hezekiah's birth or accession. In the former view we hold it quite possible that he composed those lines to lighten his heart from the heaviness of regret and dismay over the idolatrous enormities of the princely child's father, Ahaz, and the general state of irreligion which then prevailed, as well as the general distress into which this monarch had plunged the country; see especially 2 Chron. XXIX. 8, 9. To the new-born prince he attaches his fond hope of a thorough religious and moral improvement, as well as the bright vision of regenerated power, glory and welfare, which characterized traditionally the time of David's reign, alleged and believed to have been exemplary in all those respects. At the same time he magnified the portraiture of his princely subject, overdrawing it upon the model of a previous prophecy.

Let us bring what appears to us a very striking analogy of prophetic exaltation of a great person connected with his birth. It is from Virgil's Eclogues, IV. The poet hails the birth of a son to the new consul, Pollio, who had after a long and fierce intestine strife and intense misery of the Roman people brought about the peace of Brundusium, in B. C. 40. He recognizes this nativity as a propitious omen that the father's consulate was designed to usher in the "great year," with a new and better physical order of things. By this great year was meant the imagined re-birth of the whole universe according to the Platonic and Stoic mystical notion prevalent in Rome, (ibid. 4, 5). With that notion of a universal character there was combined the particular one of a Roman national cycle, according to which there was a brilliant prospect of the golden, Saturnian age returning, the wretched iron age being then believed, as it would appear from ibid. 6-10, to be drawing to its close. Virgil holds out the assurance that the new-born son will once rule in his father's place, and adorned with his father's virtues, over a peaceful Roman world (ibid. 17). The earth will offer to him—as a sign of the advent of the golden age—various spontaneously grown products; goats will give freely their milk, and they will no more, either, fear the big lions; serpents and poisonous plants will have been entirely taken away from the earth. When advancing in years the boy will witness around him a rich fertility of the soil and an abundant, even miraculous, production from it. In his manhood the earth will bring forth everything spontaneously, and there will be no more need of agricultural toil, etc.

This blessed and splendid era the poet is confident was decreed by Fate and already coming on apace, judging, as he observes, by a certain mysterious vibration of the universe which he claims to feel, as being indicative of "all things rejoicing over the arrival of the (golden) age" (ib. 52).

In connection with this allegation from Virgil we mention that it has been frequently suggested that the Isaianic passage in question may have crept into some books of the manifold Sibylline literature, and that

Presages of a Coming Golden Era of Peace. 137

Virgil may have partially adopted the motive and coloring of that charming fiction from this widely recognized prophetic source. This is indeed all the more possible as he directly refers in that very eclogue to the Cumean Sibyl, then the most renowned. We cannot discuss our point at greater length. Enough to have shown a very suggestive analogy from another literature of affixing glowing promises to a new-born child from the higher rank of society. By it the supposition will admittedly gain stronger ground, that the prophetic lines discussed may have originated at the early date of Hezekiah's birth.

Still another proposition as to the probable date of that prophetic utterance of Isaiah we will bring forward. It is much more to our mind and inclines us to urge it as deserving definite acceptance. It is, that we may safely refer the composition to a point of time soon after Ahaz' death and his son, Hezekiah's, succession. It may upon this premise well fit into the occasion of this young king's ardent and zealous stir and effort to cleanse away the base disorder and pollutions which his unworthy father had indulged and made common by his depraved example, and to restore the national religion again in its purity. This was to the prophet an assurance that better days were at hand for Judah. God, his thought was, would under such improved religious conditions of the nation take pity and remove the darkness of Assyrian oppression from the land (see ibid. IX. 1) and cause by it great rejoicing to his people (v. 2); he would interfere for them with his miraculous power and "break their yoke"—that forced on them by the Assyrians—(v. 3), even annihilate the martial accouterments of this tyrannical power. These "later day" blessings would be Providentially dispensed under the new regimen of the God-endowed and God-beloved Messianic sovereign Hezekiah (vv. 5, 6).

Now if the last supposition be upheld, we may safely assume that the prophetic passage in point belongs to the earliest or at least early days of Hezekiah's reign. Yet another seeming difficulty may be raised against it in view of the phraseology, "For unto us a child is born, etc." Would such language, it may be asked, fit the Judean king who, though he was then yet in his youth or early prime of manhood, could not sensibly be called a (newly) born child any more? To resolve this difficulty we advocate the following apprehension. The prophet may have wished to present in a most solemn style and with oracular impressiveness the idea, that Jehovah's design of saving Israel and prospering them again had already been spermatically enveloped in the life of the new king when yet an infant, or, in other words, been long ago predestined in the Divine counsel. (As to the grammatical merits of the verb used in the noted clause, which come in essentially in the case, we have to refer to the subjoined note.)*

A suitable analogy of such literary form of expression can be adduced from the same above-quoted Latin poet, Virgil, in Aeneid I. 286-296. Virgil introduces there Jupiter as disclosing to his daughter, Venus, the far-off future of the Trojan-Roman

---

*Gesenius, Commentary, in loco, p. 361-363, wavers between the futuric and preterite apprehension of the verb yullad "is born." Yet he owns, nevertheless, that there can be no question that the prophet attached his fond and strong hope to Hezekiah, when yet a lad, as the ideal king coming.

Presages of a Coming Golden Era of Peace. 139

race, the pith of which oracle is the celebration of the birth of Caesar (Augustus) and the glory and bliss of his reign. With the nativity of this Caesar whose "empire will be bounded only by the Ocean and whose fame will reach to the stars," the hard ages will grow mild, as wars will then have come to an end and be abolished. The ancient "faith" (also in the sense of truth and honor), domestic virtues and harmonious wise government will prevail (again). The dread gates of war (the gates of the temple of Janus, which were since Numa customarily open in time of war) will be firmly and tightly closed, and "within (the temple) the wicked fury (of war), sitting upon the fierce arms and bound fast with brazen chains, will rage frightfully with its bloody jaws."

Now it seems quite reasonable to suppose that Virgil gave forth those panegyric lines when his high patron, the emperor Augustus, had really given good, solid promise of a peaceful reign. Indeed were the war gates closed at his order twice during his reign, in B. C. 29 and 25.* Such auspicious condition had not happened for over two centuries previous. The Roman world seemed placated in either one of those two years, and Virgil may at one of these particular points of time have written and dedicated that alleged oracle to his adored imperial patron. He may himself have had and nursed the illusion bodied forth in the oracle. The Julian one-man rule may really have inspired his imagination with the fascinating perspective that an era of peace was ahead of the Roman nation. Weary with the past civil struggles and the mutual contests of the political leaders of Rome, he with all the better people of his nation no doubt longed anxiously for the golden era of peace and prosperity which legend had always held in store for some future times. Virgil may have fancied to see it dawn, even break soon after the accession of the new Caesar. Or, it may be, he intended by that graceful imagery merely to flatter his sovereign in his distinguished office of court-poet.

May we not consistently infer that a similar origin can be ascribed to Isaiah's rapturous lines of ch. IX. 1-6, and also to those so closely related to them, ch. XI. 1-9? They resemble Virgil's pretended oracle so very much. Both are alike in the prediction of unbounded dominion and endless peace—the happy state of the ideal era to come. (This the Romans connected with the mythical Saturnian age of the dim past, and believed in as re-prospective in the historical period of the Empire. The prophets of Israel referred it, now expressly and now tacitly, to the Jehovah-disposed indefinite "latter" or "later days.")

The time and occasion for the composition of Isaiah's noted verses suggest themselves as having been the earliest or at least the earlier part of Hezekiah's reign, when this monarch was putting forth such commendable zeal for pure religion.* It can at that particular

---

*Modern criticism has brought forward some very grave adverse opinions on the traditional piety of king Hezekiah. As disputing the spontaneity of his pious zeal, we mention Stade and Winckler. The former (in his 'History, etc.') avers that his remarkable religious reformation can "scarcely be set down as referrible to the beginning of Hezekiah's reign, but explains itself naturally as a result of the sudden deliverance from Sennacherib's onset, under the invasion of B. C. 701." Stade contends that until this fortunate occurrence, idolatry

time not have been very much to set the prophet's heart aglow with ardent admiration for his king, and inspire him to make a vivid portrait of the ideal State administered by an ideal ruler, in a word, a Messianic portrait. The essential motive for it was none other than to celebrate the reigning king, Hezekiah. For the idea once justified in his mind and conscience of apprehending and setting out this highly merited, pious monarch as the representative of such idealistic promise, it could not have been long in being seized upon by his poetic muse as well. The muse impelled him, indeed, to delineate the superb traits of his beloved royal friend as those of a real Messiah. But he practically did so only by the way of suggestion, presenting the happy and glorious state with its all-excelling ruler as *to be*. The

---

existed among the Judeans. He even charges that Hezekiah countenanced the abominable institution of Topheth, inaugurated by his father, Ahaz. This he would infer from Isa. XXX. 33. The king's puritan religiousness and practical efforts at a thorough reform of worship he puts as late as that happy deliverance, which must have wrought a radical change in his mind and sentiment. About the same view is held by Winckler (l. c.).

Sayce, too, determines upon a late date of Hezekiah's reformation, yet construes it much more creditably to him. "When Sennacherib threatened Jerusalem," he says in 'The Times of Isaiah,' "the reforms of Hezekiah were but just accomplished, etc." Now the position of the two first-named critics we must pronounce as utterly inadmissible. Even Sayce's view appears untenable in the face of this unquestioned fact, which refutes on the whole all antagonistic judgments on the pious temper of the Judean king, Hezekiah. We refer to the invitation which the latter sent to the people of the Ephraimite kingdom to take active part in the Jerusalemite Passover celebration (see 2 Chr. XXX. 1-11). The genuineness of this account cannot be disputed. It leaves no doubt, either, that

real personage to be rendered in the picture retreated into the back-ground under the careful touch of his graphic pen. For his purpose was obviously to withhold the subject of his poetic exaltation from the distinct ken of the public, though in his own vision this subject stood out in a most vital and solid shape.

His heart was closely wrapt up in that of his great royal friend. He had likely been Hezekiah's mentor and tutor in his childhood and earlier youth, and was possibly at the time of composing the glorifying lines, Judean court-prophet (compare on this Kuenen, l. c. p. 29), a court-prophet, though, who would not "cringe around the throne," but aim sincerely and strenuously to support it with his best religious and political counsel. The current "far off" notion, fondly cherished also by himself, of a coming era of happiness under the "prince

---

it happened before the fall of Samaria (B. C. 722-720). The partial transjordanic deportation of Israelites of that kingdom under Tiglath-Pileser (see 2 Kings XV. 29) had indeed, according to an express reference to it in that passage of Chr. (vv. 6-10), been a matter of the past at the time of that invitation. Yet the fatal issue of Samaria's fall was yet unaccomplished: see ibid. v. 6. Is this not a conclusive and convincing proof that Hezekiah's reform movement fell in the beginning of his reign, and most likely in its year, just as the writer of Chronicles reports?

We consider it too curious that such eminent scholars as Stade, Winckler and Sayce should have overlooked or purposely ignored the patent evidence we just produced, an evidence completely vindicating the Biblical traditions of Hezekiah's true and active piety. It proves indisputably that he had set forth for the holy task of religious reformation from his own mind and a spontaneous motive; also that the reformation itself is to be referred to the earliest period of his reign.

Presages of a Coming Golden Era of Peace. 143

of peace," with his boundless might and majesty, was bodied forth accordingly in the verses of ch. IX. 1-6, the identification of Hezekiah with it having been all but expressly personal. This era the prophet held doubtless near enough at hand to feel it in his warm imagination as already present: it was at all events to be gradually accomplished yet under Hezekiah's principate.

The figures used both in those verses and in ch. XI. 1-9, answered no doubt to his surpassing appreciation of the beloved prince's worth and Messianic qualification. These he could all the more magnify as he fixed in his prophecy upon the vague mode of intimation. Intimation allows in all instances, of good and evil alike, an almost unlimited scope of exaggeration. As well as cowardly malice may intrench itself safely behind the guard of impersonality and then, with impunity, give vent to bitter abuse or sharp invective, so may an exaltation to extreme proportions screen itself from the charge of personal fawning, so apt to be made by discerning outsiders, under the cloak of indirect address: the difference being, of course, that in the latter case the end in view is a ready discovery by the subject of the flattery, while in the former a total secrecy as to the subject of the scorn is the only safeguard.

Now the intimation Isaiah chose we hold to have been akin to that employed by Virgil. It consisted in introducing an oracle pretended to have been vouchsafed in the past. In both writers the intermingling of three tenses, the past, present and future, by a mysterious bound from an imaginary past to the application in the present, which was, again, future at the time of the alleged original revelation, characterizes the poetic utterances. Those three tenses blend in Isaiah in the verb of the clause, "For unto us a child is born" (ch. IX. 6). This expression in the uncertain Hebrew tense of its verb, oscillating, as it may be considered to be, between the future and past (see previous note page 138) receives under our proposed construction even a triple character as to tenses employed and understood. By the turn the prophet, as we take it, gave to the alleged revelation of the past in literarily divulging it for the first time so late as the period of Hezekiah's actual reign, viz., "For unto us a child will be born," there is created a threefold sense and tense, past, present and future.*

---

*We remark that alike the futuric sense of the entire discourse of ch. IX. 1-6, and its allusion to Hezekiah, become the more apparent and well-nigh assured, as we turn our attention to the analogue of Isa. XIV. 29. The illustration this passage yields we consider as of inestimable exegetical value. Its purport is a prophetic address to the Philistines, bearing the express date of the year of Ahaz' death: "Rejoice not thou, whole Palestina, because the rod of him that smote thee is broken (referring to the incursions for conquest under king Ahaz and the temporary independence from Judah thus gained; see 2 Chr. XXVIII. 18): for out of the serpent's root shall come forth a cockatrice, and his fruit shall be a fiery flying serpent." That no other but Ahaz' son and successor, Hezekiah, is here meant, admits of no question. The image under which he is represented is, that he came from a "root." This is a phraseology similar to that of ch. XI. 1. The verb yetse "shall come forth" is in the future tense proper, whereas the sprout—Hezekiah— was already on the active scene of life and government, ready at any moment, as the prophet held doubtless before his mind, to effect a deadly sting. He did effect it, too, as we learn from 2 Kings XVIII. 8. The futuric expression has here evidently the meaning of the present, with the turn of an immediately impending occurrence.

The same construction is, we hold, to be put on the term weyatsa "shall come forth," in ch. XI. 1. It is grammatically

Presages of a Coming Golden Era of Peace. 145

All this was, we surmise, resorted to that it might subserve his single and lofty purpose of representing Hezekiah as the personificator of the Messianic idea as he conceived it.

Let us say that in all probability the outward conditions in the earlier period of Hezekiah's reign corresponded to the glorious Messianic estimate of it held by the prophet. Prosperity signalized his reign from his accession to his ill-advised unfortunate revolt against Assyria under Sennacherib. This interval, perhaps in its entire length, was well adapted for Isaiah's idealistic descriptions in the dual formula of ch. IX. and XI. Stade, in his 'History of the People of Israel,' repudiating the Assyriologist assumption of any anti-Assyrian attempt having been made by Hezekiah

converted into bearing a future sense, which would even, judging by its direct consecution upon ch. X. 34, be commanded from this internal evidence (see Gesenius, in loco). The "coming forth" is, then, oscillating between the present and the future. But, on the other hand, it has to be borne in mind, that in neither passage the sprout was actually one to be generated. It existed already. The futuric form is in both instances chosen merely to indicate a relative *impending action*. Now this 'sprout,' whether under the one figure of ch. XIV. 29, or the other of ch. XI. 1, is to be understood as no other than Hezekiah. He was, is, and will be, respectively, what the prophet designed him to be. And it is for this reason that the tenses must in such discourse not be pressed too closely.

An additional support to our assumption that in both places king Hezekiah is alluded to, we find in this circumstance. In the contexts of both passages the assurance is given to the "poor," those wretched ones of society, figuring in Scripture so often as violently treated and trodden down by the powerful wealthy, that under the forthcoming sprout (as ruler) they would meet with fair consideration and dealing.

till that later revolt, suggests that not only was Judea in all that interval free from grave disturbances, it even enjoyed a marked degree of happy development and expansion—a state which could easily be taken as symptomatic of the Messianic bliss traditionally expected for the future. Sagaciously Stade derives from Isa. II. 7, that in those years of domestic tranquillity and welfare, Hezekiah could even think of increasing his military power.

But whether or no this supposition is really to be traced in the quoted passage, this much seems very probable, that prosperity characterized the Judean affairs during all the interval between Hezekiah's accession and the turbulence and catastrophe of the Assyrian invasion.*

To this whole intervening time a composition like that of the remarkable passages of Isa. IX. and XI., can fairly be held suitable, if we view them in the light of an exaggerated reflection of the happy aspect of the times—an apprehension we think so very justifiable.

According to Stade, fourteen years intervened from the beginning of Hezekiah's reign to Sennacherib's invading campaign, in 701 B. C. Other writers bring his accession, as already noted before, much farther up. This would give us a still ampler time, to the whole range of which that dual composition may reasonably be referred.

---

*That the "early years" of Hezekiah's reign "appear to have been very prosperous," is also Rawlinson's view, in 'The Kings of Israel and Judah.' He refers for it, among other passages, to these more weighty ones: 2 Kings XVIII. 7; XX. 12-15; 2 Chron. XXXII. 27-30; XXXI. 5 sq.

That Hezekiah was once during this interval involved in a warfare with the Philistines (2 Kings XVIII. 8), cannot be regarded as standing out validly against the assumption that prosperity then dominated in the Judean land. For this contest may have been only of a short duration, or it was possibly, as Winckler (l. c. p. 220) maintains, not even waged with all Philistine principalities. Again, such adversaries as the Palestinian nationalities, were, in the prophet's eyes at least, not big and dangerous enough to cause any serious alarm to the Judean nation (compare Isa. XI. 14, and see above p. 55). They were to him, according to the expressions of the latter verse, no match at all for Israel, especially if it should fall to the task of the all-powerful Messiah to deal with them, and more especially in the view, that Jehovah would always be disposed to render aid to his people against those neighboring foes, if they should prove worthy of it—a view so strongly held and repeatedly affirmed by Isaiah. Furthermore, as Hezekiah is reported to have been successful in that campaign, having "smitten" the Philistines, this warlike incident could not consistently appear to Isaiah as a real interruption of the even run of domestic welfare under Hezekiah.

Of much more consequence were, indeed, the grinding tributary relations to Assyria, which were certainly a most dispiriting offset against the peaceful and happy aspect which Judah had otherwise offered in those days.

To be sure, while smarting under this hard yoke of tributary dependence, peace and welfare were not complete, however flourishing, in all other respects, the domestic institutions of Judah may then have been.

This dependence was trying and vexatious enough to depress the spirits of even the strongest optimists among the Judeans. Yet Isaiah excelled in regard to this most troublesome and cheerless political condition of the country. It could not irritate, warm and noble patriot though he was, his balance of mind. He remained calm and untroubled, and wished and urged his people to be so, too, in the firm reliance in God's ever ready assistance. It did in no manner disturb his buoyant outlook for a bright future. For is not everything possible to Jehovah, the Almighty? He can and will—this is our interpretation of ver. 3 in Isa. IX. (see above p. 137)— break that hard and degrading yoke, which pressed so heavily upon his people, and was so ominously and obstructively in the way of their true welfare and the prospective verification of the inherited and Scripturally inherent promise of Messianic bliss and power.*

---

*This interpretation is perfectly admissible from a Hebrew grammatical point of view. For it is notorious that in the prophetical diction the past tense may have as well a future,as it ordinarily has a past and a present meaning interchangeably. This is borne out by internal evidences. See Gesenius, 'Lehrgebäude' p. 764. In the present instance it is yet particularly confirmed by the following noteworthy circumstance. We refer to Isa. X. 27. This passage is a most significant and at the same time illustrative counterpart of ver. 3 in question. Contents and bearing are in both places substantially the same. Yet in the former the prophet employs the real future tense. Is this not conclusive enough that the verb in ch. IX. 3, too, was meant in the future sense? As to the identity of meaning in both passages, it is clear beyond any dispute. In either passage the idea is given forth that it is anxiously expected, that Jehovah will deal effectually with the cruelly oppressive Assyrian king, and in a supernaturally catastrophic way. The latter is shown by the reference

Presages of a Coming Golden Era of Peace. 149

And he will, too, accomplish it—under such a pious ruler as king Hezekiah.

Probably, too, the prophet assigned in his mental vision the partial execution of this Providential catastrophe to the Messianic king—his own Messianic king, Hezekiah. A close co-operation of the Messiah in the Divine procedure is always presupposed in the prophets.

Now this consummation, doubtless the very crown of Israel's fond longing for the great Messianic future, we hold to be obscurely indicated in ch. IX. 1-6, and that, too, as we construe it by the way of analogy to the Aeneid (l. c.), under the allegation that the event had

---

in both chapters to Jehovah's astounding intercession for his people against the Midianites of old (see Judges VII.) By this reference the prophet seeks to support his hope that God would now once more vouchsafe a sudden, miraculous interference for his people, to deliver them from their present tyrannical over-lord, the Assyrian. Fire—Jehovah's own peculiar essence—is this time held in view in the prophet's imagination for the destruction of the ruthless oppressor.

We are yet to remark that our above-presented apprehension of ch. IX. 3, can not only be made out in a grammatical respect, it is even provably conformable to Isaiah's religious principle and mode of reflection. This was, the avoidance of all imprudent and rash attempts at human self-help, when it has to set itself against a superior worldly power, as was the case in the relation of Judah with the Assyrian over-lord. In all such plights a passive attitude, with a pious waiting upon Jehovah's assistance and relief was the only wise and right proceeding. See especially Isa. XXX. 15. The theory is that of non-resistance—only with a strong and intense religious base.

Accordingly, we deem it proper to add in this place, that to speak of Isaiah's "soldier-spirit," as Hackmann (quoted by Cheyne, 'Introd., etc.') does, is a downright misrepresentation of the prophet's true character.

been predestined by the Deity already when the "child was born" (or even earlier)—this having now for the first time been prophetically disclosed. That Isaiah quite confidently looked forward to such consummation we have no doubt. He would, consistently with his profound piety and trust in God, base such expectation on the king's own pious devotion, so exemplarily manifested in the restoration of the pure worship of Jehovah.

The beatific vision of the prophet was not realized. While he was "dreaming the dream and held it true," he certainly derived from it a deep delight and soothing of soul. Yet the happy enlargement and splendor of the Messianic time failed to appear. Hezekiah did not turn out to be the Messiah. Instead of enlargement, there came curtailment of territory (this, however, only on the faith of Assyrian documents). The idealistic figures of Isa. ch. IX. 5, 6, remained unverified. They may at best be classed as psychical facts, present to the prophet's ardent imagination, while "rapt into future times." Yet Assur was so much stronger than Isaiah's fiction, and fiction will never stand its ground when fronted by and matched with hard fate.

A foretaste of Messiahdom, only, the Judeans had during Hezekiah's reign, and that in the prosperity which prevailed till the calamitous Assyrian invasion. In this respect, too, it is measurably true what an eminent Rabbi of the fourth century C. E., Hillel, is reported to have openly avowed: "There is no Messiah to come more, as Israel enjoyed him (his blessings) already in the days of Hezekiah" (Talmud, treatise Synhedrin f. 98; compare ibid. f. 94, and Berachoth f. 28). Yet it was only a brief span of Messianic bliss.

The following blight of the Assyrian invasion must have taken away the impression of gratification and delight that happy condition had wrought upon the minds of the Judeans. The nations did not, either, stream in mass to Jerusalem, his seat of government, much less did they become subservient to his rule. Far from it. He himself became again, as the result of Sennacherib's invasion, Assyria's tributary and remained such till the end of his life. Nor did under him, or from his time on, the nations quit their mutual contests. Warfare with its manifold atrocities, its incalculable destruction of life and property, went on in the world as before. The clash of arms between impassioned nations has not even been brought to an end at the present highly enlightened period of the outgoing nineteenth century.

But, let us say as we close, would it really have been a boon for humanity, if with Hezekiah the line of the Jewish Messiahs had been opened, to end no more in all the succeeding history of the world? Would a one-man rule with his throne established in Jerusalem have been a real blessing to the human family? This, and this alone, is the important question. We negative it. Frankly we declare that it was so much more desirable, even already in the earlier civilization of Isaiah's time, that the Gentile nations should with the Judeans become friendly fellow-members of the "Federation of the world," than feudal dependents on a would-be Messianic ruler.

Such fellow-members all humanity should indeed be. All men should feel themselves bound together by the true sentiment of human brotherhood, with law as king to rule and direct life. Law as Messiah is good enough for all humanity and at all time: one imperative law, organic for all earthly pilgrims, who walk along the same high-road of life, share in common in the struggle for existence, as well as in the end on earth, mortality. This law is, the eternal principles and precepts of righteousness and love. In such combination as this, law may safely be trusted with imperial governance, joined, as it must be, with the faith in one God, as the all-controlling supreme Power. In his service all men shall devotedly stand, feeling themselves equals and one—in the grave sense of duty to promote the best, blessed ends of society.

www.ingramcontent.com/pod-product-compliance
Lightning Source LLC
Chambersburg PA
CBHW030252170426
43202CB00009B/714